JONAH:

What's Your Whale?

A Bible Study by Marvin Kananen

ISBN: 13: 9781530114405
ISBN: 10: 1530114403

Chapter 3, "The Book of Jonah, Author's Expanded Version"
appeared previously in a slightly different form in the author's
*Bad Theology: Short Stories Meant to Shake the Rigid and
Challenge the Spineless*. This book is available on-line.

Dedicated to the many who have accompanied me on my life's
journey.
This book is based on the first sermon I ever gave, thirty years
ago
at the Christian Family of God Church,
Arlington, Washington
and to the 2010 October Men's Retreat
of the Saint Andrew's Men's Group
from Saint Andrew's Lutheran Church, Bellevue, WA,
and all points between, before, and after.
We journey together.

Cover Photo by the Author

Jonah: What's Your Whale?
Introduction

The Book of Jonah is both one of the best known and least known books of the Bible. Everyone knows about Jonah and the whale, but that's only three verses in the book. The actual story of Jonah is a brief and early episode in the life of a prophet, a man whose later works are spoken of only in Second Kings. The story itself is not a prophecy. Over time, it has been simplified so often and in so many ways that he is now portrayed as little more than a cartoon figure. But the truth remains; what you heard in Sunday School or in the comics is not the same Jonah you're going to read about here.

This isn't your old Jonah. This isn't the story your pastor, priest, rabbi, or Sunday School teacher taught you. It remains the same four-chapter, forty-eight verse story, but there is a difference. This is not a book about the Old Testament prophet who found himself in a whale; instead this is a story about you.

You are the new Jonah. This is a story about relationship: it is the relationship between you and your whale. The Bible calls it a great fish; we'll talk about that later, but for now think whale when you hear the phrase "Great Fish." This book doesn't explain who or what your whale is: you know that for yourself. The purpose of this book is to show that we are all Jonahs and that we all have whales lurking in our histories. Sometimes the whale is an addiction, sometimes a person, most often our whales are things others cannot imagine. Some whales are kept as a secret and some are much too public.

Personally, my whale was alcohol in any form. Sober now for many years, I think of Jonah and see myself trapped inside a clear glass, bottle-shaped whale as I tried, in vain, to claw my way out. Without God, neither Jonah nor I would have been able to escape from our whales. But this isn't a book about an alcoholic finding sobriety, this is a story about you recognizing your whale. Usually it will only take a few moments of thought before you realize who or what your whale is. We cannot use the past tense here: we don't have to think about who or what the whale was. It's always in the present tense because it's always present in our lives.

My wife grew up the youngest of nine children in an almost ideal family situation on a Minnesota rural farm; her parents were wonderful. Her loving father, a model of Christian faith, is her whale, for though he is long departed from this life, she still finds joy in striving to please him even though he was proud of almost everything she ever did. His presence and his approval are like shadows that follow her in everything she does, haunting and blessing her. For her entire live she has sought to please those she recognizes as having authority over her, be they leaders, mentors, or friends.

She never woke up wondering where she was and what happened to her shoes or wallet. Her whale is nicer than mine.

A few years after college, my wife took a job at the Lutheran Bible Institute-Seattle. She taught there for over twenty years before moving into administration. As time allowed, we began teaching at our home church. We called our classroom sessions "The Jean and Marvin Theology and Heresy Lutheran Comedy Hour." We used the words "theology" and "heresy" implying she taught theology and I taught heresy, but that isn't accurate. Closer to the truth would be to say she taught the Torah, the book of law, while I taught the Talmud (Gemara), interpretations based on the Torah. She taught as closely and as accurately as she could to tell exactly what the bible story said; I read between the lines and expanded the horizons to beyond where the theologians would have been uncomfortable going. This does not bother me.

You may want to consider this book a poor cousin of a Talmudic interpretation of the Book of Jonah.

Contents

JONAH

WHAT'S YOUR WHALE?

A Spiritual Examination of Jonah

by Marvin Kananen

Chapter One
JONAH in the KJV

I recommend that you first read the following text; it is the four-chapter, forty-eight verse, 1,364-word Book of Jonah taken from the King James Version of the Bible. The King James is used here because it is in public domain, meaning we don't have to apply for any permission to quote the word of God. Another reason to read the King James Version is that I think it does not soften the blows of truth that many of the modern translations offer us as a new "Word of God." The King James Bible is written at a twelfth-grade reading level; most modern translations target the sixth or seventh grade reading levels.

I find it interesting that the Old Testament Book of Jonah is the thirty-second book of the thirty-nine books in the Old Testament, located between Obadiah (the shortest book in the Old Testament) and Micah. It is the fifth of the twelve Minor Prophets, the books that conclude the Old Testament. In the Hebrew Bible, Jonah is seventeenth of the thirty-six books (they have a single book of Samuel, Kings, and Chronicles). The Catholic Old Testament has forty-six books, of which Jonah is the thirty-ninth but it remains fifth of the twelve Minor Prophets. The Catholic version of the Old Testament also includes the historical books of Tobit, Judith, 1 Maccabees, 2 Maccabees, Sirach, Baruch, and Wisdom, thus bringing their total to forty-six books.

Jonah

King James Version

CHAPTER ONE

Now the word of the LORD came unto Jonah the son of Amittai, saying,

2 "Arise, go to Nineveh, that great city, and cry against it; for their wickedness is come up before me."

3 But Jonah rose up to flee unto Tarshish from the presence of the LORD, and went down to Joppa; and he found a ship going to Tarshish: so he paid the fare thereof, and went down into it, to go with them unto Tarshish from the presence of the LORD.

4 But the LORD sent out a great wind into the sea, and there was a mighty tempest in the sea, so that the ship was like to be broken.

5 Then the mariners were afraid, and cried every man unto his god, and cast forth the wares that were in the ship into the sea, to lighten it of them. But Jonah was gone down into the sides of the ship; and he lay, and was fast asleep.

6 So the shipmaster came to him, and said unto him, "What meanest thou, O sleeper? arise, call upon

thy God, if so be that God will think upon us, that we perish not."

7 And they said every one to his fellow, "Come, and let us cast lots, that we may know for whose cause this evil is upon us." So they cast lots, and the lot fell upon Jonah.

8 Then said they unto him, "Tell us, we pray thee, for whose cause this evil is upon us; what is thine occupation? and whence comest thou? what is thy country? and of what people art thou?"

9 And he said unto them, "I am an Hebrew; and I fear the LORD, the God of heaven, which hath made the sea and the dry land."

10 Then were the men exceedingly afraid, and said unto him. "Why hast thou done this?" For the men knew that he fled from the presence of the LORD, because he had told them.

11 Then said they unto him, "What shall we do unto thee, that the sea may be calm unto us?" for the sea wrought, and was tempestuous.

12 And he said unto them, "Take me up, and cast me forth into the sea; so shall the sea be calm unto you: for I know that for my sake this great tempest is upon you."

13 Nevertheless the men rowed hard to bring it to the land; but they could not: for the sea wrought, and was tempestuous against them.

14 Wherefore they cried unto the LORD, and said, "We beseech thee, O LORD, we beseech thee, let us not perish for this man's life, and lay not upon us innocent blood: for thou, O LORD, hast done as it pleased thee."

15 So they look up Jonah, and cast him forth into the sea: and the sea ceased from her raging.

16 Then the men feared the Lᴏʀᴅ exceedingly, and offered a sacrifice unto the Lᴏʀᴅ, and made vows.

17 Now the Lᴏʀᴅ had prepared a great fish to swallow up Jonah. And Jonah was in the belly of the fish three days and three nights.

CHAPTER TWO

Then Jonah prayed unto the LORD his God out of the fish's belly,

2 And said, "I cried by reason of mine affliction unto the LORD, and he heard me; out of the belly of hell cried I, and thou heardest my voice.

3 For thou hadst cast me into the deep, in the midst of the seas; and the floods compassed me about: all thy billows and thy waves passed over me.

4 Then I said, 'I am cast out of thy sight; yet I will look again toward thy holy temple.'

5 The waters compassed me about, even to the soul: the depth closed me round about, the weeds were wrapped about my head.

6 I went down to the bottoms of the mountains; the earth with her bars was about me for ever: yet hast thou brought up my life from corruption, O LORD my God.

7 When my soul fainted within me I remembered the LORD: and my prayer came in unto thee, into thine holy temple.

8 They that observe lying vanities forsake their own mercy.

9 But I will sacrifice unto thee with the voice of thanksgiving; I will pay that that I have vowed. Salvation is of the LORD."

10 And the LORD spake unto the fish, and it vomited out Jonah upon the dry land.

CHAPTER THREE

And the word of the LORD came unto Jonah the second time, saying,

2 "Arise, go unto Nineveh, that great city, and preach unto it the preaching that I bid thee."

3 So Jonah arose, and went unto Nineveh, according to the word of the LORD. Now Nineveh was an exceeding great city of three days' journey.

4 And Jonah began to enter into the city a day's journey, and he cried, and said, "Yet forty days, and Nineveh shall be overthrown."

5 So the people of Nineveh believed God, and proclaimed a fast, and put on sackcloth, from the greatest of them even to the least of them.

6 For word came unto the king of Nineveh, and he arose from his throne, and he laid his robe from him, and covered him with sackcloth, and sat in ashes.

7 And he caused it to be proclaimed and published through Nineveh by the decree of the king and his nobles, saying, "Let neither man nor beast, herd nor flock, taste any thing: let them not feed, nor drink water:

8 But let man and beast be covered with sackcloth, and cry mightily unto God: yea, let them turn every one from his evil way, and from the violence that is in their hands.

9 Who can tell if God will turn and repent, and turn away from his fierce anger, that we perish not?"

10 And God saw their works, that they turned from their evil way; and God repented of the evil, that he had said that he would do unto them; and he did it not.

CHAPTER FOUR

But it displeased Jonah exceedingly, and he was very angry.

2 And he prayed unto the LORD, and said, "I pray thee, O LORD, was not this my saying, when I was yet in my country? Therefore I fled before unto Tarshish: for I knew that thou art a gracious God, and merciful, slow to anger, and of great kindness, and repentest thee of the evil.

3 Therefore now, O LORD, take, I beseech thee, my life from me; for it is better for me to die than to live."

4 Then said the LORD, "Doest thou well to be angry?"

5 So Jonah went out of the city, and sat on the east side of the city, and there made him a booth, and sat under it in the shadow, till he might see what would become of the city.

6 And the LORD God prepared a gourd, and made it to come up over Jonah, that it might be a shadow over his head, to deliver him from his grief. So Jonah was exceeding glad of the gourd.

7 But God prepared a worm when the morning rose the next day, and it smote the gourd that it withered.

8 And it came to pass, when the sun did arise, that God prepared a vehement east wind; and the sun beat upon the head of Jonah, that he fainted, and wished in himself to die, and said, It is better for me to die than to live.

9 And God said to Jonah, "Doest thou well to be angry for the gourd?" And he said, "I do well to be angry, even unto death."

10 Then said the LORD, "Thou hast had pity on the gourd, for the which thou hast not laboured, neither madest it grow; which came up in a night, and perished in a night: 11 And should not I spare Nineveh, that great city, wherein are more then sixscore thousand persons that cannot discern between their right hand and their left hand; and also much cattle?"

Chapter Two

Your Favorite Bible Version

Chapter Two of this book is not found here. The second chapter is found in your favorite version of the Bible. Go to your own Bible, hopefully your favorite version, and read the Book of Jonah again. It'll be the same short story and yet different.

It is important that you feel comfortable with the Jonah story because in Chapter Three of this book, we're going to read another version of it. The third time, it'll be the Book of Jonah according to the author of this book. So go, find your version. I'm sure it's fewer than 1,500 words. Be familiar with the story because soon we'll be on unfamiliar ground, in places that are half my imagination and half found only by reading between the lines.

Chapter Three

JONAH as it's not in the KJV

I offer here another version of the book of Jonah with the assurance that of all the translations you might read, none will be less accurate than this. This is "my" Jonah—the story I mentally recite to myself whenever I read the words of any translation. My version is that of the storyteller who tells the story but does not write it. My version is not marred with theology or academic profundities; it is merely a simple tale told by a fool who dearly loves this story. My tale, 5,000 words long, goes thus:

Jonah

I know Jonah very well. I know him better than I should. He was a man much like myself who, in times of prayer, with hands raised up, assured God that he belonged wholly and solely to God. Any task God chose for him to do, he would do. He said in his heart, but never aloud, so no one else would ever hear, "You are lucky, my God, to have one such as myself, who worships you, adores you, and serves you so faithfully. I have followed the words in scripture where it says I must feed the needy, clothe the ill clothed, and visit the sick and widows and orphans and those whose life has treated them harshly, even the prisoners and the aged. God, I have given drink to those who thirsted (although never alcohol to those who craved alcohol) and I have tithed, more than tithed, of the abundance by which you have blessed me. I am truly blessed, and so I bless others. And God, LORD God, if you have any need of me, whatever it is, I will do it! For you alone have made me a mighty man of God."

As he prayed, Jonah swayed back and forth, marveling at the wonderful and devoted person he was.

For years his prayers had risen to God and for years God listened to them. It continued until the day when God spoke to Jonah. It happened this way: one day, while Jonah was praying, the Word of the LORD came to him and said, "Jonah."

The word of God comes with much punctuation. When he heard his name, Jonah heard the question mark after the name, making his name an inquiry, as he heard the exclamation mark, the period, and the other question marks that asked about the level of his commitment. Jonah heard only one word, but in it he heard a hundred questions and punctuation points that showed how far he had fallen short of being the wonderful man of God he claimed to be. Jonah heard his name and in hearing it was humbled, thus he answered hesitantly, "Yes?" He answered with one word that sounded like a simple, timid question, sounding like, "Yes?"

Like a rumble of thunder echoing from a distance, Jonah heard the voice of God say, "Arise. Go to Nineveh, that great city, and cry against it, for their wickedness has come up before me." Then, there was silence. The Talmud says God spoke with a voice that sounded like the cooing of doves. However, what Jonah heard and felt was more like lightning that had struck nearby, causing his ears were to ring as if from a crack of thunder.

The sky was clear, the day unchanged, but in that instant Jonah was changed. He knew his prayers had been heard. He knew that his God understood the kind of person Jonah truly was. There was wrapped in that word an ugly truth that Jonah heard when God revealed the divine pronunciation of his name.

"Jonah?!?..?!...!?;?!.!!!??" God spoke and Jonah knew it was pure truth. He was not the hero in God's army as he'd imagined himself to be. He was not the general to lead many souls forth into glorious battle for the LORD. He knew he was a flawed, egotistical mortal who God chose to mock with his invitation to go to Nineveh. After his name came the instructions, clear and simple, "Arise. Go . . ."

Jonah rose as God said to do. He left his hometown of Gath-hepher and made his way to Joppa. As coincidence would have it (coincidence here being what those who do not know God might call His intervention), there was a ship ready to sail immediately, and, as luck would have it, was sailing the full length of the Mediterranean Sea to Tarshish in distant Spain. The captain of the vessel may have been surprised to have a paying passenger show up at the last minute, but his fare meant more money. The passenger didn't even dicker about the price. It was a good deal for everyone: Jonah got away from God immediately and the boat made more profit.

The captain knew that Jonah was a man of class and not a thief or runaway slave, for he was a gentleman with a genteel carriage about him. When Jonah immediately went below deck rather than pausing to watch the debarkation, the captain may have assumed, "Ah, the gentleman is well used to traveling." But Jonah was not being casual; he was hiding lest any of his neighbors or family should see him and ask of his intent. He had assumed God didn't really care, but he did not want to be embarrassed by difficult questions from others who might know him.

It was the sailor's season, for a trans-Mediterranean voyage would have been unthinkable at any other time of year. The day was beautiful; conditions were perfect. The little ship slipped out of Joppa and headed due west, riding the winds off the desert. This was the sailors' moment of bliss, setting sail in ideal conditions.

Only a few hours out, a chill swept over the ship. The sun was blocked by a little cloud that should have soon passed, but it did not. Instead, the cloud grew darker and more intense until it blotted out the sun completely. The sailors, ever vigilant to any changes in the weather, noted the strangeness of the storm, even before it struck.

And strike it did, with a vengeance. In a flash of lightning and the clap of thunder, the storm was upon them, tossing the little ship. The decks were awash with the crashing waves. From the first instant the storm struck, the ship was on the verge of breaking up. The sailors knew to be afraid, for this mighty tempest was too intense. They called, each to his own god, asking for mercy. When no answer came, they threw the cargo overboard. They worked for merchants; their livelihood depended on their delivering the payloads, and yet they quickly cast off that merchandise which now threatened to weigh the ship down. Their quickness to jettison the cargo tells us how intense the storm was.

It was a desperate act, the abandoning of their cargo, but the sailors had no choice. Each wave washed over the ship and only slowly did the boat right itself and rise from beneath the waters. Death was imminent and the sailors were now struggling to survive. The wealth to be gained from their cargo no longer mattered to them.

Then one of the crew noticed that only a short way away, to the south, the wind did not seem to be blowing and the rains were not falling. The same view was revealed to the north, east, and west. They were in a mighty storm, while around them the day was calm and pleasant. They only needed to reach the calm water and they'd be safe.

The captain, taking a head count to be certain that no one was washed overboard, counted all his crew and only then realized that Jonah was not to be seen. He bravely crossed the deck and climbed down into the hold, and there he found Jonah asleep, unaware of the terror outside. He kicked him, barely hard enough to do more than wake him, and yelled to him above the din of the storm, "What does this mean, you sleeper? Aren't you aware that we are on the verge of dying? Call to your god, maybe he can save us!"

Jonah awoke in a far different world than that which he'd been in when he laid down to rest.

He had gone to sleep in the secure knowledge that he was safe. Jonah had considered God with no more regard or respect than he showed in his dealings with men. But at the instant the captain called him, Jonah realized he was wrong. When he awoke in the darkness to hear the roaring wind, felt the ship shuddering beneath him, and saw the fearful look in the eyes of the captain, he knew his God a little better. Jonah understood, at that moment, God was not going to let him escape and that the LORD God was the most terrifying thing that existed, for He was a God who cared about everything and everyone. He kept track of even a fleeing worm like Jonah.

The sailors on deck, wise to the ways of the sea, knew this was no natural storm, but it could only be the work of an angry god. A superstitious crew, the sailors huddled together and cast lots to determine who was causing this evil to fall upon them. The lot fell to Jonah. They rolled their dice, threw their bones, dealt their cards, or however they did it, and every time they threw their lots, the answer came up the same: Jonah. The stranger, the new man, was the cause of the storm.

Awake now and unable to stay below deck with the storm raging, Jonah came on deck and felt every eye on him. I can imagine one of the braver sailors coming forward to ask Jonah, "Sir, we would have you tell us why this devilish storm has befallen us. We wish to know what your occupation is and where you came from, what is your country, and from what people have you come?"

Jonah, knowing he was the source of their problems and aware that they knew he was at fault, told them straightforwardly, "I am a Hebrew, one who fears the LORD, the God of heaven, who has made both the sea and the dry lands."

The crewmen were sorry to hear his answer, for they had just sailed from Israel and knew its story. They had apparently learned the God of Israel protected His chosen people. They had seen the people and their reverence to a specific God. Now they knew it was this Hebrew on board who had brought the wrath of his God to bear upon them. Rightly, they were afraid. They asked him, "Why have you done this thing to us?"

Jonah told them everything. He told them he had chosen their boat quite by accident in which to flee from his God. He told them the full story. When he had finished confessing his guilt, they asked him what they should do. They wanted to live. Their only chance was to calm the sea, and they understood only the God of the Hebrews could quiet those troubled waters. They asked, "What shall we do with you, that the sea might calm for us?"

A man, face to face with God's judgment of him, does not lie. Jonah said, "Pick me up and throw me into the sea, for only then will the sea grow calm for you. For I know that it is my fault that this great storm is upon you." Having spoken those words, Jonah raised his hands to his face and covered his mouth, that no more words of truth might escape him. The words he uttered were not the words he meant to say, those words had popped out of his mouth.

But they did not throw him into the sea. Good men, they tried to save him and themselves by rowing to the tantalizingly close calm waters. They fought, but any progress they made forward was erased as the ship slid backward from the next wave. They struggled, they rowed, but they made no progress. The storm did not abate. They knew the Hebrew God would never allow them to escape with Jonah.

Finally, yielding to the inevitable, they themselves turned to the Lord God of Israel and cried out, "We beg of you, O Lord, we beg you to not allow us to perish for the sins of this man. Do not lay upon us the blood of this one who is innocent in our eyes, for we know it is you, Lord, who has done as you see fit."

Having spoken, they gathered around Jonah and took him up, one man at his hands, one man at his feet, and they began to swing him. "One," they all cried out; "Two," they cried out; and with the word "Three," they let him go, to sail through the air, backward, away from the ship. Even as he was in midair, the sea began to cease her raging. But Jonah, the man they had thrown overboard, did not hit the waters. As the sailors watched in awe, the waters parted, and a great sea creature rose up and swallowed Jonah before their eyes, snatching him out of the air. The sailors, lining the side of the ship, watched the broad gray back of the beast rising from the water and then diving down, until the tail fluke, as wide as the ship, passed over their heads. The fish was even bigger than their ship. Then, more suddenly than it began, it was over.

The sun broke through the clouds, bringing drying warmth. The waves slid away and were no more. The wind grew silent and, in moments, all was well. The day was suddenly calm and beautiful again while the battered ship, having jettisoned its cargo, was still afloat. The sailors who had seen what happened feared the God of the Hebrews. They offered sacrifices unto Him and they made unnamed vows, for they had caught a glimpse of the power of this God, this one God of the Hebrews. They were right to be afraid.

The ship's sails were ripped; the boat was in disarray. They rowed back to Joppa, able to pick up most of the cargo they had jettisoned. They returned to the town they'd left only a few hours before. Everyone in the port gathered to see them limp in, marveling that anyone had survived so long at sea in such a beaten condition. None of the sailors told them the storm had been just offshore. They each went to the synagogue and asked the rabbis to tell them of this God of the Israelites.

Jonah, thrown from the ship, sailed backward. He was expecting to get wet; he barely saw the mouth close over him, and then he began to slide downward on his back along a silken slide, headfirst into hell, into the stomach of the great fish, the whale.

The book calls it a great fish, an understandable description of a whale from a people of the desert. But what was a whale doing in the Mediterranean Sea? That question leads to the tale of Seymour.

INTERLUDE: The Whale

In the Arctic Ocean that year, there was a young whale named Seymour who burned with a strange desire to see more of the world than the little straits of Norway and the islands which others called Greenland and Iceland. Greenland was covered with ice, Iceland had some trees, but those subtleties were lost to Seymour. All he wanted to do was see more of this world. At first he coaxed a few of his cronies to travel with him, but by the Hebrides near Scotland the others turned back. Seymour would not turn back, he continued south. He swam until the waters got warmer and he began to feel ill. Realizing that he had been stupid long enough but had proven his point, Seymour decided to return home, but at that moment a blast of water hit him from the east. "I will go into this river until it ends, then return home and tell my family I've been to the end of the world," Seymour told himself. Then he began to swim east, into this strangest of rivers. He swam past a great rock island, and pushed on. For days he swam on, feeling sicker each day as the water grew warmer and saltier. "I am foolish," he reminded himself daily, but he was also stubborn and so he swam on. Finally, his digestive juices no longer working, ill and a little dizzy, Seymour thought he needed to belch. Rising to the surface, he let out a roar which would have pleased any young whale, and at that moment something soft and wiggly landed in his mouth and slid, still wiggling, into his stomach. It was not what a sick whale wanted.

Jonah

Jonah knew he was dead. He slid into Sheol, the land where the dead dwell. He slid on his back, headfirst down death's long tube and splashed into a vat of diluted stomach acid. He bobbed to the surface to find he only had a few inches of air in which to breathe. It smelled terrible in there, like dead fish and rotted seaweed, some of which was wrapped around his face. It was as black as can ever be found in the deepest pits of the earth. Worse than the smell was the heat, nearly 106 degrees. Worse than the heat was the sound, for he was located just beneath the whale's four hundred pound heart. Jonah heard each heart beat as if his head were inside of a kettledrum. It was worse than anything Jonah could have imagined.

"So, this is death," he reasoned. In the slimy, hot, and dark waters, floating in a slightly acidic sea while breathing in repugnant fumes. Overhead, the heart of Hades assaulted his ears. Jonah resigned himself to that fate he had earned when he had begged God to use him. He knew his sin occurred when he tried to flee instead of going to Nineveh when God invited him to work for the kingdom.

"So, this is death," he marveled again and again to himself, amazed how badly death smelled. For a day he mourned his fate and his actions. He knew his guilt was because he had displeased God. "So, this is death," he said again to himself; each time he repeated the phrase he tried to deny it. His head ached from the pounding of the great heart above him.

After two days, Jonah began to laugh.

Jonah laughed because he realized that he was not dead, but that he was still within the reach of his God. His God alone could get him out. In recognizing that fact, Jonah realized that if he was still alive, God had kept him alive for a purpose. If God had saved him, Jonah knew that God would rescue him somehow.

We can be pretty sure the prayer in the second chapter of Jonah was not written in the belly of the whale, but afterward.

INTERLUDE: The Whale

Seymour got sicker. "I'm going to die here!" the young whale marveled to himself. To die so young and far from home seemed very sad. To die alone, knowing his family would never know what happened to him, made him even sadder. At that moment, a shudder passed through his body. Seymour knew he was about to vomit, a fairly rare thing for a whale to do.

A second tremor passed through his massive body, and another, and another, and another. Suddenly, as the water grew shallow, the whale couldn't take any more of that abuse and he rose to the surface. The whale felt a roiling in his belly, and as he touched the eastern end of the Mediterranean Sea, he purged himself. His entire belly was full of bad acid; even the squiggly thing shot out through his throat, landing on the sand and into the full heat of the day.

Instantly, Seymour felt better. He knew it was time to return, for he had gone as far east as any whale was ever going to go. He was free to go home. He knew he wouldn't mention the wiggly thing when he told others about his adventure.

Jonah

From inside the belly of the whale, Jonah prayed, although his prayer was not recorded until after he was out of the whale. When he finally did write it down, he must have done so from memory. He wrote, "I cried by the reason of my affliction unto the LORD, and he heard me. From the belly of hell, I cried, and God heard my voice. For you, O LORD, had cast me into the deeps, into the middle of the sea, and the waves washed over me. I knew I was removed from your sight; yet, in time, I realized I would again see your holy temple."

This was the image: Jonah, being thrown overboard by the reluctant crew, knew he was going to die in the middle of the sea. Even as he soared backward through the air, Jonah resolved that as soon as he was under water he would exhale and then breathe in the water, that death would come quickly. That he did not get wet, but instead found himself sliding down a long tube, came as a surprise. As soon as his face emerged from the whale's stomach juices and he inhaled that rancid air, in the total blackness, in the heat, beneath the pounding heart, Jonah knew he was dead. He knew he was in the depths of Sheol, what we call hell. He accepted his fate. He waited. He had not needed to inhale the water.

He waited and he waited. It was on the morning of the third day he began to laugh, for it was then he realized he wasn't dead yet but that he was still under the watchful eye of the LORD God. Knowing that his God was faithful, Jonah also knew God still had plans for him. From the belly of that whale, in the middle of the darkness and heat and stench and sound, Jonah began to laugh because God had not forgotten him. This is why he prayed, "Even as the waters about me, to the depths of my soul, and weeds were wrapped around my head, and I was at the bottom of the mountain and the earth had bars about me like whale's ribs. Yet you, O LORD my God, brought my life from this corruption. And, remembering you, my LORD, my soul fainted and I knew my prayers, even yet, will rise up to you in your holy temple."

With those words, Jonah delivered the line in his prayers that God had waited to hear from him. Jonah said, "They who observe their own lying vanities forsake their right to any mercy." For this was Jonah's sin: his lying vanities. This was the revelation of truth that God gave to Jonah by offering him time to meditate in the whale's belly. It marked the point when Jonah, a self-proclaimed man of God, became a servant of God.

After he prophesied against himself, he was fit to offer prophecy against others. He concluded his prayer, "I will sacrifice unto God with a voice of thanksgiving. I will pay that which I have promised. Salvation is of the LORD." His vow had been to do whatever God said. It was then that God told him, for a second time, to go to Nineveh. Jonah would now keep that vow which he had once tried to ignore.

With that promise delivered, with the understanding gained, God touched the whale and the great beast "vomited out Jonah unto dry land."

Jonah, immediately after his confession, felt the surge of the whale's body as it began the regurgitation process. Waves of the contents of the whale's belly washed over Jonah, again and again, as the whale's body sought to eliminate the squirming thing that was causing it such grief. Again the body surged, again the waves washed over Jonah. Suddenly the whale straightened and Jonah was carried forth. Looking up, Jonah saw the first light in days as he saw the light at the end of the tunnel coming toward him at a high rate of speed. He was launched from the whale: he had been delivered.

Thus, he found himself on the shore in a pool of whale puke, probably bleached white from the ineffectual stomach acid of the ill leviathan, smelling like his former environment, looking like a madman. His hair stood on end, thick with juices and whitened by the acids. Jonah, standing knee deep in whale vomit, dropped to his knees and raised his hands to his God, saying, "I will do as you bid me to do!"

The word of the LORD came to Jonah again, telling him, "Arise, go to Nineveh, that great city, and preach what I tell you to preach."

Without bothering to clean himself, Jonah sloshed his way out of the disgusting pool of fluids and began the journey to Nineveh. He had no fear of thieves, for all who saw him fled before his apparition-like appearance. He crossed the wasteland and came to the great city of Nineveh, a city so vast that it took three days to walk around or so crowded that it took three days to walk every street of it.

Into that great city Jonah marched, looking like no man had ever looked before. To each resident he encountered, yelling with a voice carved from his own rage for being so delivered to perform this task for a people he despised, Jonah pointed his finger into each face and cried, in a voice mixed with glee and vengeance, "You're gonna die! In forty days this city, this Nineveh, will be brought to nothing!"

Each person who heard those words felt the anger and wrath of Jonah and recognized this man spoke the truth. The people believed Jonah, for they knew that only a God-driven man could be such a prophet. They proclaimed a fast, put on sackcloth, and began to repent.

When the king of Nineveh heard what was happening among the people of his city, he thought he should see this Israelite madman himself, and so he donned the clothes of an average person and slipped out of the palace to secretly observe Jonah. From the background he watched Jonah, but suddenly Jonah stopped, turned to the king, pointed his finger directly at him, and cried out, "God has decreed Nineveh would be overthrown, and you, you will perish, for you have been an insult to God!" Then Jonah laughed, clapped his hands, and danced in glee. Jonah wanted them all to die.

As with everyone before him, the words cut into the king's heart with the sharpness that only truth possesses. He fled Jonah, went back to his throne, and took off his disguise. Rather than dress again as a king, he covered himself with sackcloth and sat in ashes. The king repented. He proclaimed a fast throughout Nineveh that the king and the nobles, all people and animals, all herds, would fast, neither eating nor drinking. The king decreed that each beast would also be covered with sackcloth and that all who were able should cry to God, yes, the God of Jonah, and repent. All were to change their ways, to do no more evil and cease from the acts of violence which they daily committed.

The king reasoned that perhaps the God of Jonah might have a change of heart and turn from this fierce anger, and thus the city and its people might not perish.

So it happened that God did look upon them and what they were doing, how they had turned from their evil ways, and God smiled upon them. God "repented of the evil" planned for them and God gave them another chance.

While the people rejoiced, Jonah grew black in his rage. He was angry almost beyond words, for God had made the prophet look like a fool. Jonah turned his words away from the people of Nineveh, bringing them with equal force, instead speaking to God, saying, "I pray to you, O LORD, was this not what I knew you would do? Before I even left home, I knew you wouldn't do it! I tried to flee from this assignment so that you wouldn't look foolish. I knew you were too gracious to destroy this evil people, for you are merciful, too slow to anger and too kind. I knew you would repent of this task. Now, I beg of you, O LORD, to take my life!"

Jonah chose death over looking foolish. He had gone through trials no other person had ever endured, he had faithfully brought the message God had instructed him to tell the people, and now Jonah felt that God had failed him publicly and personally. Despite Jonah's promise, speaking the words God had given him to speak, Nineveh remained unharmed. Jonah felt he was the laughingstock of Nineveh. He had been faithful to God, but now the people of that city could laugh at him.

"Jonah," God spoke to him, asking, "Is it right that you are this angry, angry enough to die?"

Jonah didn't answer, in his rage he turned and marched outside the city, going east. On a hill overlooking the city, he made a place to sit beneath some shelter from the sun. He sat waiting for God to either destroy the city as He had promised or for God to destroy him.

In heaven, God looked upon Jonah and smiled again, but this time He shook His head, because Jonah was an obstinate student. God had a plant prepared, a plant that grew quickly and provided shade for Jonah's head. As the sun moved across the sky, the plant followed, always with a shadow to protect the prophet's head from the deadly rays of the desert sun.

Recognizing this plant as an embodiment of the honored recognition he truly deserved, Jonah rejoiced and was happy. But on the dawning of the fortieth day, the day when Nineveh ought to have been destroyed, God sent a worm. The worm ate the root of the plant; the plant withered. The sun rose upon Jonah that morning, and from the desert a "vehement east wind" blew. Jonah knew no one could live in those conditions; he chose to die rather than face the ridicule of the pagans of Nineveh.

"It is better for me if I die than if I live," Jonah declared aloud, as would a judge issuing a final decree against him.

"Is it right that you are angry about the gourd?" God asked Jonah. When someone smiling speaks, the listener can hear the smile. Jonah heard the smile in God's voice when He spoke.

"It is right!" Jonah screamed in self-righteousness. "I do well to be angry, even unto my own death!" Jonah could not see that his role in Nineveh had been the same as the plant's role in Jonah's life, for Jonah was still living in his world of self-centered vanities.

God is a teacher. God has lesson plans we cannot imagine and reasons and goals we do not know. God teaches us more than we could ever learn on our own. In this case, God, the teacher, said to Jonah, "Interesting, you had pity on this plant for which you did nothing, you did not plant or water it, you did not make it grow. You did nothing and, yet, when it rose in a single night, you were glad for it. When it sheltered you from the sun, you rejoiced. Why can you not be as happy for Nineveh, that great city, which I did not destroy? There are sixty thousand people there, as well as their livestock, who owe their lives to you, because you did my work! Rejoice, Jonah, and live."

And Jonah lived. He heeded God, and then he returned home. In time, he became known as one of the great prophets of his day.

Chapter Four:
Considering Jonah, Section One

1^{1}Now the word of the Lord came unto Jonah the son of Amittai saying,"...

The story of Jonah takes place about 800 B.C. during the reign of Jeroboam II, a king of Northern Israel. Jonah was born to the tribe of Asher.

Most of the books I've read on Jonah define the two Hebrew names found in the first verse, Jonah and Amattai, as meaning, "Dove" and "Truth." The writers of those commentaries like it that the meaning of Jonah's name is given as the "Dove," linking it (rightfully so) with the winged creature seen as a symbol of the Holy Spirit. This image appears a number of times throughout the Bible, examples being the role the dove played in the Noah's Ark story and as the dove descended to the newly baptized Jesus.

Jonah's father, Amattai, the meaning of whose name includes "True" or "Truth," is seen simplistically as making Jonah, the Dove, to be the son of the Truth. It's really a pleasant package of names and pleasing to the listener. We will pause in our story and examine the names found in the first verse in the Book of Jonah.

These writers of the commentaries I've read seem to have taken their meanings for these names from the definitions provided by James Strong (1822-1894) in *Strongs' Exhaustive Concordance* (1890). But understand this: *Strong's* is not a dictionary, it is a word index that merely offers a gloss, or minimalist interpretation, in the place of a real definition. With that understood, let us consider the name "Jonah" as found in *Strong's*. There you can read in the mistitled "Hebrew and Chaldee Dictionary" (It's not a dictionary!) section of the concordance, noting the numbers shown in italics refer to the Hebrew section of Strong's Hebrew and Chaldee section and non-italicized numbers refer to the Greek section. Here we start with #3124 (it's Jonas in the Greek, #2495):

Strong's Hebrew reads:
#3124: **Yonah**, *yo-naw'*; the same as *3123*; *Jonah*, an Isr.:—Jonah.
We go to the previously mentioned number, #3123, where we read:
#3123: **yownah**, *yo-naw'*; prob. from the same as *3196*; a *dove* (appr. from the *warmth* of their mating):—dove, pigeon.

Leaping to *#3196*:

#3196: **yayin**, *yah'-yin*; from an unused root mean. to *effervesce*; *wine* (as fermented); by impl. *intoxication*:—banqueting, wine, wine[-bibber].

The Greek reads:

#2495: **Ionas**, ee-o-nas'; of Heb. or. [*#3124*] *Jonas* (i.e. *Jonah*), the name of two Isr.:—Jonas.

There is something far more emotive if, rather than thinking of Jonah's name simply meaning "Dove," we think of the mood which is post-coital in nature with a slight effervescent effect from wine, resting in one's own warmth in the fellowship of a lover as taken from *3123* above. This is the Jonah we want to consider when we think of him, and truly not the Holy Spirit in the form of a dove. One is the very proper Holy Spirit of God; the other is quite human, laid back in bed, sexually satisfied, craving a cigarette and living a moment, warm and content and thoroughly worldly. Restating that, one is a bidder to do the LORD's bidding and the other is a bibber, still in a slightly drunk state and a smugly successful lover.

In like fashion, regarding his father's name, again taken from *Strong's Exhaustive Dictionary*, let us consider the Hebrew reading:

#573: **'Amittay**, *am-it-tah'ee*; from *571*: *veracious*: *Amittai*, an Isr.:—Amittai.

We look at *571*:

#571: **'emeth**, *eh'-meth*; contr. from *539*; *stability*; fig. *certainty, truth, trustworthiness*:— assured(-ly), establishment, faithful, right, sure, true(-ly, -th), verity.

Again, we follow *Strong's #539* and consider:

#539: **'aman**, *aw-man'*; a prin. root; prop. *to build up* or *support*; to *foster* as a parent or nurse; fig. to *render* (or *be*) *firm* or faithful, to *trust* or believe, to be *permanent* or quiet; mor. to *be true* or certain; once (Isa. 30:21; by interch. for *541*) to *go to the right hand*:—hence assurance, believe, bring up, establish, + fail, be faithful (of long continuance, steadfast, sure, surely, trusty, verified), nurse(-ing father), (put), trust, turn to the right.

Amattai, a thoroughly lovely name for a parent, does not appear in the New Testament. His name appears only twice in the Old Testament: the first time in Second Kings 14:25 (²⁵He restored the coast of Israel from the entering of Hamath unto the sea of the plain, according to the word of the Lord God of Israel, which he spake by the hand of his servant **Jonah, the son of Amittai**, the prophet, which was of Gath-hepher.) and the second time in Jonah 1:1 (see above, page 37). In both cases he is identified as the father of Jonah. The strength of his name implies one who believes and serves God. It is easy to see that the son of a man so named might someday be called to be a prophet. The implication is that Jonah knew of the presence of God in his life since childhood under his father's influence. Again, considering *Strong's*, starting from the third generation gloss to the first (#*573* to #*571* to #*539*), the meaning of Amattai might be seen as one who "fosters trustworthiness veraciously." It is an interesting transliteration, but do remember that a name is not merely what you call someone, it can be a title of what that person is expected to become. Amattai is the source of today's name Emmitt.

We would probably all be better people if we lived up to the meaning of our names.

Jonah, who shows himself to be a rather pompous man, was the son of this Amattai. It would be understandable that such a father figure might be a rigid disciplinarian. Jonah's father has a name that extends back in *Strong's* to the third generation: let us consider a third generational reading of his son's name (#*3124* to #*3123* to #*3196*). If we look at the name and roots of Jonah's name with the same audacity applied to his father's name, couldn't Jonah's name also have meant "intoxicated pigeon" or "fermented dove?" For simplicity's sake, our teachers said, "His name means 'Dove!'" and went on to the story. The name deserves more attention than that.

One interesting piece of information is that a number of Jewish traditions tell that the widow woman's son who Elijah revived in I Kings 17:17-24 was actually young Jonah, whose mother was a woman of Zarephath named Tzarfati, as recorded in Sukkah 5:1. This would have meant Amattai had died early in Jonah's life and, if the story were true, also could have made Elijah to be Jonah's spiritual father and mentor. This information comes from the Talmudic writings on the Jewish Bible and not actual biblical text.

However, as I personally identify with Jonah, I'll stick with Strong's glossed definitions. I am satisfied by neither the Talmud's interesting but unlikely story of the Elijah-Jonah connection nor the safe, clean, and concise "dove" answer my pastor attempted to foist on me when I was a child. I think my pastor felt that his answer was the only truth I needed and that Jonah meant Dove. My pastor did not define Amattai for me.

With that behind us, now let us return to the story with those bits of insight into Jonah and his father and consider that there is another personality here in the first verse. Behold, it is the LORD! But this is not the Lord as if He were merely a lord of a manor, this is a title (not a name) written in all capitalized letters: LORD. But, so that we are not placated by simple capitalized letters such as are found in acronyms like UN, NAACP, or SPCA, consider the word itself and realize that the three final letters of the word, though capitalized, are shown in a slightly smaller font. There is no other word like this; it is like a name. This is the name of the LORD!

That awesome fact recognized about the word, realize that the word LORD is an English word that honors the personal name of God. LORD (note the variable fonts of capital letters) represents the English transcription of YHWH. It intentionally looks and sounds nothing like Yahweh, the name of the God to the Hebrews.

I love the name of God as it is revealed to Moses in Exodus 3:14. God, when the people of Israel were about to ask Moses who had sent him, said, in the English translation: "I AM WHO I AM." It is a name that I cannot speak, for if I said those words it would only be a counterfeit name because I am not God. When I say, "I am who I am," I am merely me, but when God said it, GOD IS! It is a bit like the moment in Exodus 7:8-13 when Moses, confronting the Pharaoh and was asked for a sign, told Aaron to throw down his staff and it became a serpent. Pharaoh turned to his magicians and demanded of them, "Do something." They threw down their sticks and their sticks then became serpents. But the staff of Aaron then consumed those other serpents and suddenly there was nothing left for the magicians to say and do, for their staffs were gone. The Pharaoh's wise men could only remain silent. So too is the name of God, for HE IS; and I am not. "I AM WHO I AM," says God and we wisely say, "Amen, Hallelujah. Amen."

This is the Lord who spoke to Jonah.

I offer another example, this one from the New Testament regarding the power of the name of God, illustrated by Jesus in the Garden of Gethsemane at the moment of his arrest. Seven times previously in the Gospel of John, Jesus had given definition of his presence, each of which further connected himself with the I AM of the Hebrew Bible and provides us with clues to his divine nature. These clues are called the "Seven Great I AMs". At various times, Jesus said, "I am" 1-"The Bread of Life" (6:35); 2-"The Light of the World" (8:12); 3-"The Gate" (10:9); 4-"The Good Shepherd" (10:11); 5-"The Resurrection and the Life" (11:25-26);

6-"The Way, the Truth, and the Light" (14:6); and 7-"The Vine" (15:5).

There is an eighth occurrence in the Gospel of John where Jesus uses the "I AM" in a divine sense. We pick up the story in the Garden of Gethsemane where we read in the Gospel of John 18, starting with verse 3:

3 Judas then, having received a band of men and officers from the chief priests and Pharisees, cometh thither with lanterns and torches and weapons.
4 Jesus therefore, knowing all things that should come upon him, went forth, and said unto them, Whom seek ye?
5 They answered him, Jesus of Nazareth. Jesus saith unto them, **I am he**. And Judas also, which betrayed him, stood with them.
6 As soon then as he had said unto them, **I am he**, they went backward, and fell to the ground.
7 Then asked he them again, Whom seek ye ? And they said, Jesus of Nazareth.
8 Jesus answered, I have told you that **I am he**: if therefore ye seek me, let these go their way:
9 That the saying might be fulfilled, which he spake, Of them which thou gavest me have I lost none.

When they came to arrest him, Jesus asked them who it was they sought. They answered that they were looking for Jesus of Nazareth. When he said, "I AM HE," the first time he answered, he may have used the divine name. Probably no different than would happen to us today if we heard Jesus say that name, they fell back and did not understand they had fallen. They got up, probably a bit confused, and Jesus asked them again, "Who do you seek?" They repeated themselves, although perhaps a little more timidly as they knocked the leaves and dirt from their clothes, and answered the question, "Jesus of Nazareth." Jesus responded a second time, but this time when he said, "I am he," they did not fall. I imagine they didn't fall the second time because he spoke the words in the language of the day and did not use the divine force encapsulated in the name of God: I AM WHO I AM.

We call him LORD, but the name of God that comes down to us is actually YHWH, a very old Hebrew name. Before creation, YHWH was. Before Adam arose from the red clay and stood, the name YHWH was. The Jews believe that the name YHWH is so holy that mortals should never try to pronounce it. When the text calls for YHWH to be read aloud, the Jewish reader pronounces the Hebrew word for the name of the LORD, "Adonai." Adonai cannot be considered a proper name; it is a title that means "my lord" or "my master." This is the name used over six thousand times in the Hebrew Bible. By speaking this title and not God's name, over time the correct pronunciation of God's personal name has vanished. God's name, thoroughly honored and holy, will never again be correctly pronounced by mortals.

An interesting side note here is that the altering

of the pronunciation of a word is not generally made by changing the consonants but by affecting the vowel sounds. Vowel sounds, though sometimes thought to be constant, never are. There is no better way to protect a word or name from being correctly pronounced than by removing its vowel sounds. Thus we get the Hebrew name of God as the famous Tetragrammaton YHWH. As if to further protect the pronunciation, the early Hebrew scholars took the vowel sounds of Adonai, a different word, and reapplied them to YHWH, a particularly brilliant move to obscure the pronunciation. Now, when later Biblical readers saw the name YHWH, they concluded that the word YHWH was pronounced as Jehovah (at least since the word "Jehovah" was introduced in English first as *Iehouah* and later as *Jehovah* by William Tyndale [1494-1536]).

Trying to show an example of how this works in English, it might be like trying to pronounce the word "BND," knowing simply that the vowel sounds are absent. Thus BND could be pronounced band, bend, bind, bond, bund, bound, beaned, banned, abound, etc. with significant change in meanings.

In English the word is written as LORD. Again, please note the difference between LORD, Lord, and the specialized use of capitals in LORD. The uniqueness of the name LORD as YHWH seems to be the result of an artificial application in English of the word from the Hebrew language. The uniqueness of LORD is created to separate the word from other meanings of the word "lord." It is worth noting that the first Creed of the Christian Church uses the phrase "Jesus is Kurios," which is how the Septuagint, the original Greek

translation of the Old Testament (300 B.C.), translated
YHWH. This was a confession that Jesus is YHWH! The
true etymology of YHWH will forever remain unclear
and will always be subject to debate. The mystery
behind the etymology of the word "LORD" is quite
clearly intentional; its intent is honorable.

Without going into greater detail, here is what
Strong's tells us of the name of the LORD:

3068: **'Yᵉhovih**, *yeh-ho-vaw'*; from *1961*;
(the) self-*Existent* or Eternal; *Jehovah*, Jewish
national name of God:—Jehovah, the Lord.
Comp. *3050*, *3069*.

Before we compare the words, let us follow
Strong's path to *1961*:

1961: **hayah**, *haw-yaw'*; a prim. root [comp.
1933]; to *exist*, i.e. *be* or *become, come to pass*
(always emphatic, and not a mere copula or
auxiliary):—beacon X altogether, be(-come,
accomplished, committed, like), break, cause,
come (to pass), do, faint, fall, + follow, happen, X
have, last, pertain, quit (one-) self, require, X use.

1933: **hava'**, *haw-vaw'*; or **havah**, *haw-
vaw'*; a prim. root [comp. *183*, *1961*] supposed to
mean prop. to *breathe*; to *be* (in the sense of
existence):—be, X have.

We glance briefly at *183*:

183: **'avah**, *aw-vaw'*; a prim. root; to wish
for:—covet, (greatly) desire, be desirous, long,
lust (after).

Then we will go back to the opening gloss *3068* {see above} and follow it to *Strong's 3050*:

3050: **'Yahh**, *yaw*; contr. for *3068*, and mean. the same; *Jah*, the sacred name:—Jah, the Lord, most vehement. Cp. names to "-iah," "-jah."

This leads us to the YHWH to Adonai glosses:

3069: **'Yᵉhovih**, *yeh-ho-vee'*; a var. of *3068* (used after *136*, and pronounced by Jews as *430*, in order to prevent the repetition of the same sound, since they elsewhere pronounce *3068* as *136*):—God.

136: **'Adonay**, *ad-o-noy'*; an emphatic form of *113*; the *Lord* (used as a prop. name of God only):—(my) Lord.

113: **'adown**, *aw-done'*; or (short.) **'adon**, *aw-done'*; from an unused root (mean. to rule); *sovereign*, i.e. *controller* (human or divine):—lord, master, owner. Comp. also names beginning with "Adoni-".

This leads us to the Elohim glosses:

430: **'elohiym**, *el-o-heem'*; plur of *433*; *gods* in the ordinary sense; but spec. used (in the plur. thus, esp. with the art.) of the supreme *God*; occasionally applied by way of deference to *magistrates*; and sometimes as a superlative:—angels, X exceeding, God (gods) (-dess, -ly), X (very) great, judges, X mighty.

433: **'elowahh**, *el-o'-ah*; rarely (short.)
'eloahh, *el-o'-ah*; prob. prol. (emphat.) from *410*;
a *deity* or the *Deity*:—God; god. See *430* [see
above].

410: **'el**, *ale*; short. from *352*; *strength*; as
adj. *mighty*; espec. the *Almighty* (but used also of
any *deity*):—God (god), X goodly, X great, idol,
might(-y one), power, strong. Comp. names in
"-el."

352: **'ayil**, *ah'-yil*; from the name as *193*,
prop. *strength*; hence anything *strong*; spec. a
chief (politically); also a *ram* (from his strength);
a *pilaster* (as a strong support); an *oak* or other
strong tree:—mighty (man), lintel, oak, post.
ram, tree.

193 **'uwl**, *ool*; from an unused root mean.
to *twist*, i.e. (by impl.) be *strong*; the *body* (as
being *rolled* together); also *powerful*:—mighty,
strength.

YHWH is the second creation name of God. In
Genesis 2:4b the Bible reads, "In the day that the LORD
God (read Adonai, think YHWH) made the earth and the
heavens, . . ." God's name changes from Elohim to
YHWH Elohim in Genesis 2:4. Chapter one spoke of
Elohim, the God who created the heavens and the earth
(Gen. 1:1), and again as the Spirit of God who was
moving on the face of the waters (Gen. 1:2).

We will make no further attempt to define "God."
God, Elohim, is used some 2,500 times in the Hebrew

Bible. It is God. It's not a name, it is God; it's what we call our God, a descriptive title at best. It is how we address, look at, and communicate with and about God.

Considering *Strong's* use of the English form the name of God, let us look anew at the meaning of the word. Derived from *Strong's* but applied with the same dashing and daring we applied to the names of Jonah and Amattai, we will consider YHWH, the name of God. He is named "He Who Is Who Is All That Is To Be." He is God, and this is the meaning of his name, but it is not his name—for the name is Holy and we will not try to pronounce it. When speaking to Jonah, it was the LORD who spoke to him.

It's good that the LORD spoke with words to Jonah, for throughout the Bible there are instances of the LORD's physical presence appearing to various peoples. Here I offer several first-person accounts with the significant words underlined. The first comes from Revelation 1:12-17):

¹²And I turned to see the voice that spake with me. And being turned, I saw seven golden candlesticks; ¹³ And in the midst of the seven candlesticks one like unto the Son of man, clothed with a garment down to the foot, and girt about the paps with a golden girdle. ¹⁴ His head and his hairs were white like wool, as white as snow; and his eyes were as a flame of fire; ¹⁵ And his feet like unto fine brass, as if they burned in a furnace; and his voice as the sound

of many waters. ¹⁶ And he had in his right hand seven stars: and out of his mouth went a sharp two-edged sword: and his countenance was as the sun shineth in his strength.

¹⁷ And when I saw him, <u>I fell at his feet as dead</u>. And he laid his right hand upon me, saying unto me, Fear not; I am the first and the last.

Or again, let us look at Ezekiel 1:28:

²⁸ As the appearance of the bow that is in the cloud in the day of rain, so was the appearance of the brightness round about. This was the appearance of the likeness of the glory of the LORD. And <u>when I saw it, I fell upon my face</u>, and I heard a voice of one that spake.

Or, Daniel 8:18

¹⁵And it came to pass, when I, even I Daniel, had seen the vision, and sought for the meaning, then, behold, there stood before me as the appearance of a man. ¹⁶And I heard a man's voice between the banks of Ulai, which called, and said, Gabriel, make this man to understand the vision.¹⁷So he came near where I stood: and when he came, I was afraid, and fell upon my face: but he said unto me, Understand, O son of man: for at the time of the end shall be the vision.

18Now as he was speaking with me, <u>I was in a deep sleep on my face</u> toward the ground: but he touched me, and set me upright.

Or, Daniel again, 10:7

7And I Daniel alone saw the vision: for the men that were with me saw not the vision; but a great quaking fell upon them, so that they fled to hide themselves. **8**Therefore I was left alone, and saw this great vision, and there remained no strength in me: for my comeliness was turned in me into corruption, and I retained no strength. **9**Yet heard I the voice of his words: and when I heard the voice of his words, then was <u>I in a deep sleep on my face, and my face toward the ground</u>. **10**And, behold, an hand touched me, which set me upon my knees and upon the palms of my hands.

There is an apparent difference between hearing the Word of God as Jonah did and actually seeing the bearer of the word, be it God himself (as with Moses) or his messengers. In the four instances cited, each time the writers saw the speaker they passed out, be it falling at his feet as dead, face down, or asleep. It makes no difference if it was shock or fear; as holy as God's name is, so is the presence of his messengers.

Jonah heard only the "Word of the LORD." Jonah never asked, "Who are thou who speakest thus?" He knew. It was the word of the LORD (again, think Adonai). Jonah knew who it was.

*   *   *

With all that as a background, now armed with as much fiction as theology, let us resume our study of the Book of Jonah and reconsider again the first verse of Jonah:

1^1 Now the word of the LORD came unto Jonah the son of Amittai, saying,

What? The LORD who created all that exists just said what? Obviously Jonah had always wanted to hear from God, the God of his father and the God of Abraham, Jacob, Isaac, Joseph, and David. But what is the infinitely profound word that God, the creator of the universe, would offer to one as faithful as Jonah had been? What blessing would God give to Jonah? God said:

^{2} Arise. Go to Nineveh, that great city, and cry against it; for their wickedness is come up before me.

We do not know what message Jonah thought he might receive from God, but it was certainly not the message he got. The first word was "Arise." The second word was "Go." Clearly this is a message of action, to arise and to go. These are the kind of words a prophet would want to hear. This was a command from God: "Arise and go . . ."

The third word rolled off God's tongue, "to," and then I can imagine a short pause in which time Jonah's mind would race in to fill the void after the preposition. Go to . . . where? Would he go to Jerusalem and bring the message of God to teach the scribes and Pharisees? Would he be called to lead his people to a new spiritual awakening that would sweep the country? Three words into the message, it was all good. "Arise. Go to . . ." are words given to missionaries, this was a call to serve the LORD!

"Nineveh." To Jonah, the word would have sounded like a crack of thunder. It was a word so heavy that Jonah couldn't breathe with that word swooning through him. Nineveh was beyond the end of the world; located in what is now northern Iraq. It was a place without hope, a murderous city. Nineveh was the last place on earth where any Jewish prophet would ever want to go. When one thinks of Nineveh, the cities of Sodom and Gomorrah should come to mind. To make matters worse, God didn't just name the city but also defined the city. God said, "Nineveh, that great city, and cry against it; for their wickedness is come up before me." The LORD said to "cry against it!" while I'm sure Jonah would have preferred to "whine against it" from a safe distance.

This was a moment of crisis that God initiated. Jonah was being sent to exactly the place where he had no desire to go. It was the worst of all assignments. It was the worst of the worst! But when the power of the Word, whether audible or not, comes forth from God, there is no room for debate, argument, and criticism. The command, an imperative, said simply "Arise. Go." When God says to do something, it is to be done immediately. When God says something "will be done," then there's a period of waiting. When God says, "Do it," the proper and only wise response is to do it immediately. God spoke neither in the past nor the future tense but in the active present tense, an imperative: "Go!"

Jonah apparently reacted immediately. Probably packing minimally to make for a quicker exit, he left his home in Gath-hepher (also written as Gittah-hepher). As a good Jew would be, he was probably married and had children, but that detail is never mentioned. What was mentioned twice was the place-name in the Hebrew Bible, once in 2 Kings, 14:25: "He restored the coast of Israel from the entering of Hamath unto the sea of the plain, according to the word of the LORD God of Israel, which he spake by the hand of his servant Jonah, the son of Amittai, the prophet, which was of **Gath-hepher**," and again in Joshua 19:13, "And from thence passeth on along on the east **to Gittah-hepher,** to Ittah-kazin, and goeth out to Remmon-methoar."

Based on *Strong's* Hebrew section, #5059, Gath here is seen in the sense of a place for the crushing of grapes as one walks in a wine vat. *Strong's 1660*, Hepher, is a verb suggesting to dig or to search for something. This is, by implication, the name of a place where the wine vat (or press) was dug into the ground. It was in such a place where Gideon was found (Judges 6:11).

We pause in our story just as Jonah is about to

take flight and consider where Jonah is from. Gath-hepher is not mentioned in the Book of Jonah, but there is no reason to doubt that it is Jonah's hometown, located in the north near the border of Zebulon. The name Gath-hepher in *Strong's Exhaustive Concordance*, Hebrew #*1662*, literally means, "wine-press of the digging." The Hebrew transliteration is Gat-hefer.

There are seven possible sites for Gath-hepher, the most accepted one is located in Galilee, now the Arab village of el-Meshed north of Nazareth and less than a mile from Cana. The supposed grave of Jonah, long a tourist site, was destroyed by terrorists in the early 21st century.

If we go back and look at the third gloss of the name Jonah as found in *Strong's*, we see that Hebrew word #*3196 ya-yin* (see, page 39) is an unused root of Jonah meaning effervescent, as in fermented wine. By that it implies the noun means *intoxication*, as referring to banqueting wine or a person considered a wine bibber (drunk). Considering the meaning of Gath-hepher, the wine press, we have an implication unfolding in the names.

After two verses we find that Jonah of the Winepress, having learned of God from his earthly father, Amittai, then hears the voice of God telling him to "Arise. Go . . ." In verse three, Jonah rises up and goes, but not in a manner pleasing to the Lord. We read:

3But Jonah rose up to flee unto Tarshish from the presence of the Lord, and went down to Joppa; and he found a ship going to Tarshish: so he paid the fare thereof, and went down into it, to go with them unto Tarshish from the presence of the LORD.

Joppa was a good location, a seaport located on the eastern edge of the Mediterranean Sea. It could have been Jonah's original intent to sail north from Joppa (current day Jaffa) to land in current day Syria and from there to begin the trek to Nineveh. It was not an unreasonable thing to imagine, but then a wondrous thing happened; the faithful and well-trained son of Amittai fled from the presence of the LORD. While it is possible that he was sailing for Tarsus in Turkey as some have tried to render the name of the city, the overwhelming number of people said it was to Tarshish he was going, a city in Spain. The trip would have been a trans-Mediterranean voyage of 2300 miles. Basically, he could not have fled any farther than Tarshish. The distance from Joppa to Nineveh would have been about 600 miles. The 300-mile sea voyage from Joppa to a port in the Antioch area would have shortened the land segment of the trip to roughly 400 miles. But that's not what Jonah wanted.

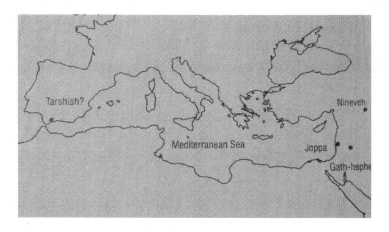

Bewildered by the sudden intrusion of the LORD into his life, Jonah decided to flee. There had been no "Get Ready" or "Get set," but Jonah's race began with the words, "Arise. Go." When the LORD said, "Arise," Jonah arose. When the LORD said, "Go," Jonah went, but he fled in the opposite direction rather than obey. Later in the book we will hear Jonah rationalize his decision to flee from the command he received from God, but in this verse we have all we need. Jonah tried to flee all the way across the Mediterranean Sea to escape "from the presence of the LORD." Twice that phrase is repeated in the single sentence with two main clauses ("to flee unto Tarshish" and in an almost duplicate use, "to go with them unto Tarshish"). Would Jonah have stopped at Tarshish, or would he have sought another boat to take him farther, perhaps to the British Isles?

Jonah did not obey God in this, but he did react to God. Perhaps, if we understood the holiness of God better, we'd also have wanted to flee. But know this: no one outwits God.

I've heard some writers claim that Jonah paid all the fares just so the boat would sail immediately. I disagree, for I believe that God, in God's timing, had the boat ready to go and the fare Jonah would have paid was only an unexpected bonus for the owner of the vessel, probably the captain. I believe that Jonah's flight to escape from the LORD 's presence was an unmentioned part of God's plan to get Jonah ready to go to Nineveh. Jonah, oblivious to anything but his escape, went down to Joppa and then down to the ship. His escape was perfectly timed; he was now free "from the presence of the LORD."

Jonah, in his desperation to get away, walked into a secondary but invisible plan of God, for God knows how easy it is to get someone do the wrong thing. All God had to do was make it easy. As we follow Jonah through the first chapter, we will find the direction he travels is constant: he goes "down" to Joppa, "down" into the ship, "down" into the sides of the ship, and later inside the great fish (which we will soon begin calling "the whale") "down" to the bottoms of the mountains. "Up" is harder; "down" is easy. Down is the direction for the lazy one or the coward. The Lord made Jonah's way coincidently easy.

Jonah was probably asleep before the ship sailed.

⁴But the Lord sent out a great wind into the sea, and there was a mighty tempest in the sea, so that the ship was like to be broken.

I love that word, "But." We can make our own plans, "But the Lord . . ." That little phrase marks the beginning of some of the greatest missional work that has ever taken place. The sailors may well have thought at first that bad luck dropped the storm on them, that coincidence happened. They would soon understand that it was not happenstance. It was "But the Lord" that descended on them. The Great Wind was sent "into the sea." The tempest is, by definition, a violent and windy storm. The storm was so strong that from the beginning it threatened to break the ship.

They would not have set sail on a day when the weather was threatening; the idea when you sail is to get as far as you can before the unforeseen weather hits you. My image is that the ship left Joppa with a great offshore breeze that would drive them west with a good hope for a short and pleasant voyage. Imagine blue sky, a few wispy clouds, a calm sea, and the promise of a successful journey. All was wonderful, "But the LORD sent out a great wind." The storm was not directed at the ship or her crew, but at Jonah who was sleeping soundly in the ship.

[5]Then the mariners were afraid, and cried every man unto his god, and cast forth the wares that were in the ship into the sea, to lighten it of them. But Jonah was gone down into the sides of the ship; and he lay, and was fast asleep.

Sailors know what the sea can do and how quickly the weather can change, and they also know what is not natural. They'd call that kind of event "Supernatural." They recognized the nature of the storm that descended upon them from on high as something special. It was supernatural.

Mariners live in a mixed zone of tension somewhere between fear and confidence; they love and hate the sea with equal intensity. The mark of experienced seamen is that they know when to be afraid. Apparently this storm hit with such violence and speed that they knew it was unnatural. How deep was their fear? It was deep enough that they "cried every man unto his god." They knew storms do not appear out of the blue, and with something as violent as the tempest that hit them, they knew the hand of a god was upon them. They didn't know which god, for they were many men, each of whom seemed to have their own gods. Each man called upon his gods. They did something next that is so awesome that we, even from a safe distance from that storm, can recognize it as being truly and horrendously frightful, a true act of desperation: they jettisoned their cargo.

Can you imagine a truck driver hitting such a storm that he would empty the contents of his vehicle on the side of the road? He'd be fired. The sailors, almost as soon as the storm hit, "cast forth the wares that were in the ship into the sea, to lighten it of them." Their cargo was the reason they were there; it represented the purpose of the ship. They threw their cargo overboard in an attempt to save the ship, for the only thing more valuable than their cargo was their own lives. If the ship broke up, especially in so major a gale, they would die. To save their lives, they lightened the ship so it might ride more easily on the waves in that most unnatural storm.

Lightening the ship may have helped somewhat, but they were still in trouble. They clung together fighting for survival. It was probably the captain himself who asked, "Has anyone seen our passenger?" They had not. Jonah had gone below deck while they were still in the harbor. It was possible he'd drowned below deck. The captain crossed the deck between waves and went down to check the fate of their passenger.

He found Jonah asleep, hidden in the hold of the ship. The captain probably wondered what kind of passenger could be so ignorant or innocent or drunk as to sleep through such a storm.

6So the shipmaster came to him, and said unto him, What meanest thou, O sleeper? arise, call upon thy God, if so be that God will think upon us, that we perish not.

I have always wondered if the captain kicked him to wake him from his deep sleep. I'm sure while he was taking his money the captain called his passenger "Sir," so he probably didn't kick him. You do not strike a paying passenger; however, I'm fairly certain the captain's attitude came out in an angry yell, demanding, "What do you mean, O sleeper? Arise." These words appear later in the Bible in Ephesians 5:14: "Awake thou that sleepest, and arise from the dead, and Christ shall give thee light."

Is everyone telling Jonah to "Arise?" God said it, now the captain offers a mock parody of the LORD's command for Jonah to "Arise and Go!" But, unlike the LORD's command to "Arise and Go," the captain, most certainly not a Hebrew, yelled to him over the roar of gale force winds and the sound of crashing waves, "Arise, and pray!" Actually, he said, "Call upon thy God, if so be that God will think upon us, that we perish not." There is no indication that Jonah actually prayed during the time of Chapter One, although he prayed intently in the following chapter.

How intense was the storm? So intense that the only hope they found was in prayer. There are times in life when situation and peril are so overwhelming that there is nothing else left for us to do. That's when the only thing remaining is to pray, to call upon God and ask for mercy. Even paying passengers are not exempt from being called to pray. There were no lifeboats, only their prayers.

The wording of the King James Bible, "O sleeper. Arise. Call upon your God," pleases me more than the words of any other translation. Various forms of those words are often heard from an irate parent, spouse, and teacher. "O sleeper, arise" are fairly negative words, and they always speak a truth that I, a frequent sleeper, don't want to face. The captain, probably a polytheist himself, said, "Call upon your God that we do not perish." He's the captain, first checking on the fate of his passenger and, upon finding him well (albeit asleep), tells him to call upon his god, unaware that his passenger's god is The God.

Reading between the lines in the story, obviously Jonah did arise and went on deck. He'd gone below with calm seas and blue sky; he came on deck into black weather, hurricane force winds, and a driving rain. Did he wonder, "How long have I been asleep?" Bewildered, except with insight into the nature of the storm, Jonah faced the sailors and the storm, knowing that he was the answer to the question that they had not yet asked. His advantage in sleeping is that there was no need to testify against himself. But then the captain woke him and changed everything.

When Jonah saw the storm, he knew it was from heaven and he knew it was raging for his sake alone.

[7]And they (the seamen) said every one to his fellow, "Come, and let us cast lots, that we may know for whose cause this evil is upon us." So

they cast lots, and the lot fell upon Jonah.

It is interesting that the sailors tried to figure out who was the "cause" and not who was at fault. This didn't involve blame or even accusation, but who was the cause of the storm. Did God cause the storm? No, Jonah did by his behavior. They answered their own question in the casting of lots.

When the world has questions for which there seem to be no answers, where do they find answers? Our newspapers carry horoscopes in which some hope to find the truth; likewise there are fortunetellers, oracles, and palm readers who promise insight. In this story the sailors cast lots. The image you may want is from Melville's novel *Moby Dick* where the tattooed cannibal, Queequeg, is casting his "runes" to see his future and discovers he is destined to die. In Jonah, the sailors cast lots in order that they might discern who was the cause of the evil that had befallen them. We will never know the nature of the lots, but we know when the sailors had cast them, they turned their eyes to Jonah.

There is a difference between the casting of lots and reading signs or omens. The casting of lots can be flipping a coin, throwing dice, I Ching, or several other methods of letting fate guide you, hopefully as Gideon's fleece (Judges 6:36-40) guided him. In the New Testament they cast lots to see who would replace Judas among the disciples (Acts 1:26). Different than casting lots, omens involve reading signs that already exist and interpreting them in an attempt to forecast the future. Until Jonah was awake and could give them answers, there was nothing else to be done. They waited.

8Then said they unto him, Tell us, we pray thee, for whose cause this evil is upon us? what is thine occupation? and whence comest thou? what is thy country? and of what people art thou?

In all, they asked Jonah eight questions, five in this verse (1-who's the cause? 2-what's your occupation? 3-from where did you come? 4-what is your country? and 5-who are your people?). The remaining three questions are found in verse 6-what meanest thou? in verse 10-why did you do this? and, finally, in verse 11-what shall we do? All the questions use the polite form of address.

The image is this: awakened from his sleep by the captain, Jonah comes up to the deck and realizes all the crewmen's eyes are on him. He is the stranger, the one probably responsible for the evil weather that has beset the little ship. They've already thrown their cargo overboard, their hope for profit gone. Now before them stood the stranger, the one the lots said was the cause of the unnatural weather. They watched him carefully, wondering what kind of man this passenger was.

They knew Jonah was fleeing something; they didn't know what or why. They asked him, "Who is the cause of the storm? What is your occupation? And where are you from, what country and what people?" Jonah, who'd been asleep, woke up in a storm at sea and was instantly accused of things that others claimed he had done. They didn't know the extent of his guilt or why the storm hit them. The storm involved the sailors personally; they wanted to know why it was happening.

⁹And he said unto them, I am an Hebrew; and I fear the LORD, the God of heaven, which hath made the sea and the dry land.

Sometimes you really don't want your questions answered. In Jonah's case, he didn't give simple answers; he offered them spiritual answers, although not in the order the questions were asked. "I am an Hebrew" is not where he was from and "I fear the LORD" does not describe his occupation. His answers were not evasive; they were answers to the questions the sailors should have asked. Jonah was honest in giving them the information they sought. He was, in fact, protecting them because Jonah knew his God could make the storm worse than that which they were already enduring.

At this point we're going to read further between the lines and guess, maybe speculate, that the crew of the boat and learned some things about the God of the Hebrews. Apparently when Jonah said, "I am an Hebrew," that struck a note in their hearts. They had probably seen things in Israel that intimidated them about the God the Hebrews served. They'd been happy with their idol poles and vague images of their gods, but now, this God, who they'd never seen or whose name they had never heard uttered, had caused the storm. Then, to their horror and to magnify the dread they already carried from their time in Israel, Jonah added, "I fear the LORD, the God of heaven, which hath made the sea and the dry land."

They had found the source of their storm. Apparently, Jonah's words were words they did not want to hear, as was shown by their reaction. Did any of the sailors wonder aloud, "Did he have to be the God of the dry land and SEA?"

10Then were the men exceedingly afraid, and said unto him. Why hast thou done this? For the men knew that he fled from the presence of the LORD, because he had told them.

What did he tell them that made them so afraid, that he feared the LORD God who made the sea and the dry land? Apparently wiser than their passenger, the sailors reasoned that if the God of the Hebrews made both the land and the sea, there was no place they could go to avoid him. To where could Jonah have been fleeing toward if it was neither on the land nor sea? Yet still, it was his presence that brought the storm upon them. Do not forget the storm; it was raging around them. Drenched from the mix of salt waves and freshwater rains, chilled by the wind, the sailors understood that if they offended Jonah's God, they were dead. If they did nothing, they were going to die. They needed an answer they did not have; no casting of lots could help them. They turned to Jonah for help.

11Then said they unto him, What shall we do unto thee, that the sea may be calm unto us? for the sea wrought, and was tempestuous.

Was there frenzy in their voices when they asked him, "What were they to do?" They asked Jonah, "What can we do for you that the sea will grow calm for us? For this sea is unnaturally angry, tempestuous, and deadly! What can we do?"

Idols seem to be placated easily by offering them some additional sacrifices, but this was no stone or wood idol they were confronting: this was the creator God.

12And he said unto them, Take me up, and cast me forth into the sea; so shall the sea be calm unto you: for I know that for my sake this great tempest is upon you. They had prayed to their gods to no avail, and they thought this Hebrew man would have insight into what they could do, but he said nothing.

He told them what they should do, and he answered them more clearly than he ever answered the LORD. To the sailors he said, "Take me up and throw me into the sea, for only then will the sea grow still." I wonder if that's what he meant to say, or did those words jump out of his mouth unintentionally. Yet he confessed, "I know this great storm has come on you because of me." It was not Jonah the sailors feared; it was Jonah's God.

The men again prayed to their own gods, hoping their gods might put this God of the Hebrews in his place and that their gods might calm the sea. Jonah did nothing to help them, he held on to stay upright in the rocking boat and watched, probably hoping that the sea would calm while knowing it wouldn't. He had given them their solution; now he could only hope they would be successful on their own and save him in the process.

¹³Nevertheless the men rowed hard to bring it to the land; but they could not: for the sea wrought, and was tempestuous against them.

There is something sweetly childish about this verse. Despite what they'd seen and heard, they still believed they could save the situation by rowing, their version of simply walking away. They hoped they could merely row back to Joppa and drop their passenger off as if nothing had happened; they could not. This is the verse where the sailors realized they were powerless before God. It took them some time to figure out that fact. They had resisted the obvious as they tried to row out of the storm, but finally they realized they couldn't do anything.

This is a telling verse. In the broad expanse of the ocean, if you man the oars it is to keep the bow of the boat into the waves, to ride the seas. But this is not what they did; instead they tried to row to land. Why? Because land was close? I wonder if the sailors looked to the south and saw the sea was calm there, and to the north it was calm, as well as the west and the east—but where they were: a wicked gale had descended upon them. They thought, using human logic, if they could but row to land they'd be safe. The sea and the storm wouldn't allow that. The story says the sea was "wrought," a word that means, "worked against them." They rowed, only to be swept back into the middle of the storm. They rowed hard and harder until the oars seemed ready to snap; still they could not get away from the storm. Many people think that if they do good things, everything will turn out right; but good is never really good enough. The sailors rowed and went nowhere. All they got out of trying to be good was exhaustion. It is a common story that continues to this day.

Their efforts, praiseworthy and honorable to consider, gained them nothing except to show them that this God of the Hebrews was truly the God of the seas, and they had no doubt he was the God of the land, as well.

14Wherefore they cried unto the LORD, and said, We beseech thee, O LORD, we beseech thee, let us not perish for this man's life, and lay not upon us innocent blood: for thou, O LORD, hast done as it pleased thee.

They called him LORD, not God. Perhaps there is some insight found in that detail: they knew to fear and revere the name of the Hebrew God.

Without success, the sailors quit their rowing and ceased praying to their gods. Instead they began to pray to Jonah's God. Probably not knowing the meaning of God's name and not aware of the significance of meaning of YHWH (Adonai), they prayed to the God of

Jonah. They besought God, they begged of God, saying, "Let us not perish for this man's life, and lay not upon us innocent blood!"

They are saying, "If we kill him, let him be guilty and do not hold us responsible. Do not let us die for his sake." They had one chance to live, and that was to do as Jonah had told them they must do: they must throw him overboard. They prayed that Jonah's powerful God would recognize their innocence and be gracious to them, for it was Jonah who was the cause of the problem.

Then, to assure Jonah's God that they were innocent, they placed the responsibility onto Jonah's God when they added, "For thou, O LORD, have done to him as it pleased you to do." "It wasn't us, it was you!" they claimed.

15So they took up Jonah, and cast him forth into the sea: and the sea ceased from her raging.

I think every book I read on the subject of Jonah was full of praise for the seamen who prayed to their gods even when there was no sign that Jonah prayed to his. They were willing to cast their cargo overboard. They tried to row out of the storm. Everything they tried came up short until they finally picked Jonah up, who they were convinced was the source of their troubles, and cast him into the sea.

In my imagination, I can picture the two biggest men in the crew grabbing Jonah, one on his legs and the other on his arms, walking to the middle of the ship, and then swinging Jonah back and forth as if he were in a hammock. "One," they might have said, then, "Two," then, "Three!" On "Three" they let him go. Backwards, he sailed into the rough seas.

Did they still doubt their own actions? Probably, but when they cast him forth the "sea ceased from her raging." Suddenly there was quietness where a storm had just been pounding savagely at them and their ship.

The waves fell flat on the surface of the water, the wind ceased, and the sun broke through the clouds. On the bare deck the sailors stood, all eyes on the waters, witnesses to the fate of their passenger. They were soaked; moments before they had been afraid they would die, and then suddenly they were in a calm sea with sunlight.

Some miracles are slow in occurring, some happen instantly.

16Then the men feared the LORD exceedingly, and offered a sacrifice unto the LORD, and made vows.

The name of their sacrifice was Jonah. The sailors had one thought: The God of Jonah IS The GOD of the Earth and Seas. They had just had an encounter with the God of All Creation. It was an event that would have caused a transformation in the heart of every man who witnessed the event. It is ease to imagine that each made a personal vow to God, the God of Jonah who created the Earth and Seas.

17Now the LORD had prepared a great fish to swallow up Jonah. And Jonah was in the belly of the fish three days and three nights.

Here my version differs from the direct, word-for-word description of the story. This is what I imagine in this scene: Without even offering him a refund on his fare, the sailors swung Jonah like a heavy sack and at the count of "Three!" they threw him in the air, over the side of the ship. But in my version Jonah never hit the water. In that instant when he was sailing backward through the air, looking back at the ship, making eye contact with the sailors one last time, the seas parted below him. A great whale appeared, its mouth open to take in air. It took in Jonah as well.

The sailors were already full of self-doubt about throwing a paying passenger overboard even though he was the one who told them to do it. They'd done as the man said and thrown him into the sea, but at that instant a huge creature (whales are rarely found in the Mediterranean Sea) emerged from the angry seas and swallowed him. The sailors would have had no doubt but that they'd done the right thing by Jonah's God.

At that moment, everyone stared as the creature re-submerged. If they hadn't had a moment of conversion before, they certainly were now willing to believe in the God of the Hebrews! They watched in awe as a creature the size of their ship slipped back under the waters.

That was when the waves fell flat, the sun broke through and the rain and wind ceased. Seconds after releasing Jonah to his fate, they were safe. I could imagine their jettisoned cargo caught in an eddy, still together and within their reach. They gathered in what they could find, reloaded the ship and sailed west, away from Israel, away from the God of such power and presence.

The sailors are never heard from again. But it would have been good to hear what they said about the day they threw a passenger into the sea only to see a great fish rise from the waters and swallow the man.

WAS IT A WHALE?

Was it a whale? We really don't know—but we have an interesting answer anyway.

Probably if the sailors had written the book, they wouldn't have used the term "great fish" because they would have heard of or perhaps seen whales, but almost certainly they would have believed in other large and dangerous creatures of the sea. However, a desert people like the Hebrews would not have had the word "whale" in their vocabulary. This author's silly example of that is to try to imagine what the ancient Hebrew word for kangaroo would have been. My assumed reply would have been something like "a large, hopping mouse." So too, was the whale. The term "big fish" is only a description; it's not ichthyology. The situation would have been made more difficult because Jonah's view of the creature had been mostly internal. We don't know what he actually saw and if he ever recognized what swallowed him.

Despite our repeated warnings not to use it as a literary resource, once again we will carefully consider *Strong's Concordance* as our reference, looking first at how the Hebrew text uses the word "fish:"

1709 **dag** *dawg*; or (fully) **da'g** (Neh. 13:16) *dawg*; from *1711*; a *fish* (as *prolific*); or perh. rather from *1672* (as *timid*); but still better from *1672* (in the sense of *squirming*, i.e. moving by the vibratory action of the tail); a *fish* (often used collect.):—fish.

Going back a generation to *1711* as directed by *Strong's*, we find:

1711 dagah *daw-gaw'*; a prim. root; *to move rapidly*; used only as a denom. from *1709*; to *spawn*, i.e. *become numerous*:—grow.

Let us consider *1672*:

1672 da'ag *daw-ag'*; a prim. root; *be anxious*:—be afraid (careful, sorry), sorrow, take thought.

There is nothing there to indicate a whale. However, the word "whale" comes to us from the third century B.C. Septuagint, the original translation of the Hebrew Bible into Greek. Then, taking the translation of that text into modern English, I offer this verse, the first set in Greek:

Jon 2:1 καὶ προσηύξατο Ιωνας πρὸς κύριον τὸν θεὸν αὐτοῦ ἐκ τῆς κοιλίας τοῦ κήτους

Here we translate the Greek, which was translated from Hebrew, into English, and read:

2^1 Now the L<small>ORD</small> had commanded a great whale to swallow up Jonas: and Jonas was in the belly of the <u>whale</u> three days and three nights.

Interestingly, their translation moves the last verse of the first chapter of Jonas (Greek for Jonah) from 1:17 to 2:1. It is from the Greeks that the word "whale" is introduced into the book, not by the Hebrews. But the Greeks didn't do it either. Had the Hebrews or the Greeks used the word "whale," our story would have been simpler. However, they didn't say, "whale," they said, again according to *Strong's* Greek:

2785 **κῆτος kētos** *kay'-tos*; prob. from the base of 5490; a huge *fish* (as *gaping* for prey):— whale.

Which sends us to:

5490 **χασμα chasma** *khas'-mah*; from a form of an obsol. prim. **χαώ chao** (to "*gape*" or "*yawn*"); a "chasm" or *vacancy* (impassable interval):—gulf.

The image is that of a great, open mouth. Was this a fish to be feared, a fish capable of easily swallowing a person or anything thrown into the sea? It is a terribly strong image. Perhaps for its squiggly motion as shown in *1709* (the Hebrew dag [*dawg*]); this leads to its root being tied to the Greek "huge fish with gaping jaws." But we're not at the word whale yet. Here it comes:

The word "whale" is an incorrect translation of the Greek κῆτος first used in Matthew 12:40 in the original King James Bible, an error which is too often carried on in later translations. But κῆτος is the name of the genus (class) of fish that, for the Greeks, included dolphins, sharks, whales, etc. It is a mix of mammals and Chondrichthyes (fish-like creatures that have a cartilaginous skeleton, e.g., sharks).

This is the truth: the word wasn't "whale," it was and will be forevermore "fish" and anyone who tells you otherwise is wrong. A whale is not a fish. However, whale is a convenient description that makes the story more comprehendible to young and old listeners. Any time you hear someone use the phrase "Jonah and the whale" you can be assured A) they don't know the accuracy of translation or else B) they are, like me, prone to telling the story simply. You will find in this book that I use "whale" in places where story overcomes the need for total accuracy. And do note, the subtitle of this book does not say, "What's Your Great Fish?" but rather "What's Your Whale?"

There is a further confusing point: three times the word "whale" appears in the King James Version of the Old Testament, so again it was the English translators who translated the "sea beast" as "whale."

In Job 7:12, we read: [12]Am I a sea, or a <u>whale</u>, that thou settest a watch over me?

In Ezekiel 32:2, we read: **2**Son of man, take up a lamentation for Pharaoh king of Egypt, and say unto him, Thou art like a young lion of the nations, and thou art as a <u>whale</u> in the seas: and thou camest forth with thy rivers, and troubledst the waters with thy feet, and fouledst their rivers.

We read in Genesis 1:21: **21**And God created great <u>whales</u>, and every living creature that moveth, which the waters brought forth abundantly, after their kind, and every winged fowl after his kind: and God saw that it was good.

Also, we need to mention Matthew 12:40 where it's not a Hebrew concept. In Matthew 12:40 (KJV) we read: **40**For as Jonas was three days and three nights in the <u>whale's</u> belly; so shall the Son of man be three days and three nights in the heart of the earth.

Chapter Four

Continued:

Considering Jonah, Section Two

We resume our story with Jonah, wet and chilly from the gale while the boat on which he rented space was not likely to survive in the storm much longer. Even with the cargo had been jettisoned, the boat could barely stay above the waves. The crew understood that Jonah's God, the God of Abraham, was after Jonah, and in final desperation they picked up Jonah and threw him into the sea. Almost instantly the storm broke. The sailors understood they had done the right thing in returning their passenger to the "God who made the seas and the dry land."

They had seen Jonah thrown into the air, but just

before he could hit the surface of the sea, the waters split and a great beast rose from beneath the ship and swallowed the man whole. The sea creature disappeared beneath the waves and the seas calmed. The sailors gathered what they could of their abandoned cargo and sailed away. For the sailors, the story ended when Jonah disappeared. It's doubtful they could have imagined that that was not the end of Jonah's story. It wasn't.

Jonah, still captive to his God, could hardly have believed his story was just beginning, but it was.

It probably seemed to Jonah that the sailors almost gently swung him by his hands and feet. He heard their "One, Two, Three" as they cast him into the air. He drew in a lungful of air and prepared to land on his back in the water, but instead a great darkness overtook him and he began to slide down a long tunnel.

"The entrance to Sheol" he may have thought as he entered the gaping mouth, meaning "the way to hell." Backward he slid down the slimy tube. Still holding his breath, he hit more slime, a small pond of it, like water in a cave. But the stuff he landed in was hot, half way between boiling and freezing points if it had been water. Sliding backward, he fought to get his head out of the pool. Jonah opened his eyes and found it was pitch black. Already slimy and uncomfortably hot when his head bobbed up to a clear zone, Jonah's face floated just above the slimy waters. When he exhaled and inhaled, he discovered it was the foulest air he'd ever smelled. And, as bad as all that was, just over him beat an incredibly large drum, the loudest he'd ever heard. The drum's pounding beat occurred about once every four seconds.

Jonah floated on his back and thought, "This is hell." He must have thought he was dead. There was nothing left for Jonah to do. He floated there and could think of nothing he could do except to pray and call for mercy from his God who had rightfully put Jonah in that tight situation.

Thus said, we return to our Bible study. In Jonah 2:1, according to the English Bible, we read:

2¹ Then Jonah prayed unto the LORD his God out of the fish's belly,

Even atheists, when they understand they are about to die, often call upon God. Those of faith do likewise. Jonah knew he was dead. All he could do was pray, and that is what he did. Perhaps he got a glimpse of the moment he was swallowed and knew he'd been eaten by a great fish, or me may have deduced where he was by the smells and heat and odors. Once inside the sea creature, there was only prayer; it was his only "weapon" and his only "hope." As once before prayer had been the sailors' only lifeboat, now it was Jonah's only recourse.

Did he know he was inside the great fish? I can imagine him gagging, slime covering his lips and his eyes, which he might as well keep shut anyway because there is no light. Jonah was in the ultimate prayer closet, and pray he did! He prayed "unto" the LORD, not "for" or "at" the LORD, but unto him. For three of the loneliest, probably longest, days of his life, he prayed. Jonah now prayed hard without a trace of hypocrisy.

It's doubtful Jonah could have prayed kneeling down. It's more likely he prayed while floating on his back in a sea that was beyond description. Now it's safe to assume that Jonah was not writing down his prayer at that moment, but he wrote it later and tried to capture the essence of what he said. This is what he wrote:

² And said, I cried by reason of mine affliction unto the Lord, and he heard me; out of the belly of hell cried I, and thou heardest my voice.

For eight consecutive verses in this ten-verse chapter (eleven in the Septuagint), Jonah prayed. I love his prayer. Too often when I pray, I pray to "My Lord and Savior" or "My God" or forms thereof, but Jonah, a man of God, said "Thou" in the King James Version, or "You" in most translations. He used the second person, personal pronoun, "You" as you might do with a friend. He said, "From here, in the belly of hell in the form of this great beast, You heard me."

I would have loved it if someone had written that word as one speaks of God as "You," with the capitalized and mixed font size as they write the word "Lord," but they do not and so neither shall I. In my heart I know he is Lord. When I speak to him, I am mentally using the You form. Listening to me, you'd never know the difference between "you," "YOU" and "You," but I do and the Lord does.

Jonah cried out. He cried out for this "reason," for this was the "reason of mine affliction." He was the cause of his affliction, and he was the reason. Truly, how do you imagine a more oppressive situation than that in which Jonah found himself? We can recognize his position, floating on his back in the sour stomach acid of a whale, in the total darkness and 106-degree heat, beneath the pounding of a heart that weighed several hundred pounds. Assuming the whale was having some digestive problems because Jonah wasn't digested in the stomach acids, the stench would have been overpowering. He was trapped; there was no place to run. Yet it was in this place, in total darkness, that the eyes of Jonah opened (figuratively) and he saw his own sinful ways. It was in the total darkness that Jonah saw the light.

Exaggerating only slightly, this is what my image is for those people who live without having God in their lives. But that's not the point of this illustration. Rather, I want you to understand that it's just to show that when it seems that all is lost, God is still there to hear our prayers.

³ For thou hadst cast me into the deep, in the midst of the seas; and the floods compassed me about: all thy billows and thy waves passed over me.

Verse three is not an accusation: it's a definition. Although it sounds tragic, there's a bit of humor in this description. "I was in the deep, in the midst of the sea with the floods surrounding me, your waves and billows pass over me." It sounds like an even worse assignment than Nineveh was. The verb with the pronoun, "you cast me" is different than if it was written "you had me cast." It shows that there was a role for the sailors to accomplish in meeting God's will. It's a fine detail that makes no difference in a "thy will be done" world, but it shows that Jonah was not accusing the LORD of throwing him into the whale's mouth. Jonah did not have to ask where he was or why he was there; he knew.

Strangely, I think Jonah found hope at this moment, in that unlikely place and time. I could picture him first in a sea of self-pity; then, after a time, Jonah started to laugh, not because his situation was funny but because he had a flash of insight into the workings of God in his life.

4 Then I said, I am cast out of thy sight; yet I will look again toward thy holy temple.

Here is an incredibly sad statement, "I am cast out of thy sight." It was probably the first moment in his life when he felt truly distant from God, and yet it was that same sense of loss that made the next statement possible. It is much like Peter when he asked Jesus later (John 6:68): "LORD, to whom shall we turn?" So did Jonah know there was no place else to turn. At the depth of his soul, he mounted the courage to offer these words of absolute faith, "Yet I will look again . . ."

Here speaks the ultimate optimist! Here is the testimony of a man who believes in God and the power of God. In a place of incredible horror, where all he had left was his memories, he remembered the LORD. He would have said something like, "Although I am where no one should ever be, beyond the vision or imagination of anyone who has ever lived and am almost completely screened from God, yet I know I will look again toward thy holy temple."

This is why Jonah could laugh. He understood that God had put him there. Yet, because he could still breathe air (albeit rancid), and even though the stomach acids of the whale were slimy, yet they did not digest him. He was alive for a purpose. If he was alive for a purpose, God still had use for him. And if God would use him even from where he now floated, God had a plan. Jonah was finally willing to let God lead.

None of the things that had befallen him were accidental or coincidental. The crew of the ship was ready to sail at that moment when Jonah walked up. Even more exact in the timing was the emergence of the whale just as Jonah was flying backwards. Jonah considered his situation and came to the conclusion that God was still with him and had never left him. He, who once thought to flee to Tarshish to escape God, had found God even in the whale's belly. Said Jonah, "Yet I will look again toward they holy temple.

5 The waters compassed me about, even to the soul: the depth closed me round about, the weeds were wrapped about my head.

From what depths can we find ourselves saved? How deep do you think we can sink and still not be found? Here is Jonah's description, offering a version of the story similar to some I've heard from drug and alcohol abusers. My addicts could easily have said, "The waters were over me, my soul knew I was dying, the depth washed over me and I was wrapped up in the images of my own depth. It was as if death had me in its grip." Yet the truth is that anyone who can speak such words can be saved, has found help, and has reached up a hand to be pulled from death. These are the words of a survivor who, finding himself in a world that felt to be without hope, still found hope and rescue and salvation.

How low was Jonah? Entrapped, probably claustrophobic, ensnared in seaweed, Jonah knew it was his disobedience that brought him to that vile place. From the lowest he'd ever been, Jonah prayed:

6 I went down to the bottoms of the mountains; the earth with her bars was about me for ever: yet hast thou brought up my life from corruption, O Lord my God.

There was never anyone lower, incarcerated in an organic prison, certainly it seemed forever—YET, YOU have brought me to life. You have freed me. You have redeemed me! Who did this? "O Lord my GOD!" Jonah was another sinner who realized his vain and pompous life was truly only a corrupt mockery of the manner of life he thought he'd been living. It was here in the prayer that Jonah offered his thanks to the God, who brought him up from his life of corruption.

When? "WHEN my soul fainted within me, I remembered the Lord!" To what depth did Jonah have to sink? Jonah descended to where his soul "fainted within me."

7 When my soul fainted within me I remembered the LORD: and my prayer came in unto thee, into thine holy temple.

For these last five verses, Jonah's prayer has told us of the depths he had reached, but in verse 8 comes the why. Why would God save such a one? God saved Jonah because Jonah understood he was a vain sinner and he confessed it.

8 They that observe lying vanities forsake their own mercy.

Here is one of the greatest lessons in the entire Bible.

Probably one of the more common errors made in people's thinking is that the citizens of the world today think the world is worse today than it ever was. They assume that people have become more egotistical and self-centered than they ever were before. But if we look in the Bible, we can see our generation today with all its sins is only a reflection of the same sins as those of our Biblical forbearers. Their sins are our sins, although sometimes our means and opportunities to sin have increased. Our lying vanities are the same as Jonah's or David's or anyone you can name in the Bible. Which do you love more, your vanity or the truth? When you look in the mirror do you see the face of someone God could love or do you look for flaws, wrinkles, imperfection?

Our vanity is astounding. Do you pay more for makeup and cologne than what you put in the church offering or give to the poor? Do you have shoes and clothes you've never worn? Do you lie about your age and weight? How vain are you? Are you as bad as I am?

Here is the great line in Jonah's prayer, "They who observe their own lying vanities have forsaken their own mercies!" Jonah so loved himself that he thought he could flee from the assignment God had given him. He did not flee because he feared God; he fled because he loved himself more. Personally, I'm sure the thought, "I have been such an idiot!" passed through his thinking while he was in the whale. He never claimed to be innocent or undeserving of his fate. His sin was that he never lived up to his words or promises.

If Jonah had not realized that it was his own "lying vanities" that got him into the whale, he probably never would have gotten out. It was in the belly of the whale where Jonah realized it wasn't his faith but his trust in God that mattered most. And best, he knew the way out: contrite prayers. He'd always had faith, now he had trust.

⁹ But I will sacrifice unto thee with the voice of thanksgiving; I will pay that that I have vowed. Salvation is of the Lord.

As the sailors vowed, so did Jonah. His vow was of obedience, not of money or sacrifice. He prayed with a "voice of thanksgiving," these are words of a person on a mission. As he had said, so now would he do, exactly as he vowed.

The first word in this verse, "But," is again the

key moment. It is a key, single-syllabled conjunction in his confession, followed immediately by two "I will" statements. The Jonah who came out of the whale was different than the one who entered. His lessons were far more valuable than a university degree, for the words he spoke were no longer of the vanity of Jonah but of his newly found honesty. The man who was described in 2 Kings 14:25 as God's "servant Jonah, the son of Amittai," was not the same man who slid backward down the gullet of the great fish. Inside the whale, he was just beginning to live up to that title: "God's servant."

"I will sacrifice my sacrifices to you with a voice of thanksgiving" no longer were words of Jonah's personal vanity and public displays. "I will pay that that I have vowed," he said, remembering how at one time he had flaunted himself as being the ideal worshipper of God, only to later find out the truth that he was really only a clown of his own vanity.

Then, he who was still in the whale said the words, "Salvation is of the LORD." Period. Who but the LORD offers salvation? No one but the LORD delivers.

And, speaking of delivery, when it was time to restore Jonah to his assigned mission, the LORD spoke to the fish. I love a God who speaks to fish.

This line is part of the reason I believe that God actually orchestrated Jonah's entire sea voyage. Everything there was too wonderfully placed to be coincidental. The timing of the boat is easier to explain than the timing of the "great fish." But the timing was there. I'm certain God arranged for a fish large enough to swallow an adult and then deliver the man to a place where he could continue the work of God that he'd been called to do. I suspect when God told the fish to release the prisoner, it wasn't the first time He'd spoken to that particular fish.

Jonah saw his flight from Joppa as a chaotic coincidence of events that proved he could never really escape God. But I doubt if Jonah ever knew that he was the object of a chain of events by which he not only arrived in Nineveh, but he arrived ready to preach the message God had sent through him. As he had once surrendered to the sailors' needs, so here he surrendered to his God. The way back to God had begun with his confession in the belly of the whale. The way to Nineveh began the second time on some un-named beach.

Had he gone directly to Nineveh from home, he'd not have been prepared. God first prepared a great fish; now God had prepared Jonah to go forth and preach.

It was at that moment, and with all the dignity Jonah had earned by his aborted flight, the great fish "vomited" Jonah onto dry land.

10 And the LORD spake unto the fish, and it vomited out Jonah upon the dry land.

I have the image of Jonah rising from a fairly large pool of whale vomit, himself slightly bleached from three days spent in some diluted but seriously raunchy stomach acid. He was as slimy as a dead fish and smelled of whale vomit. Blinded by the light after three days in the darkest imaginable situation, I wonder if Jonah ever saw the great fish back off from the shore and return to its life in the sea. Does the child see his mother at the moment of birth? Did Jonah look up before the great fish disappeared? The fish hadn't eaten him, despite what the sailors might have thought; it delivered him. The whale had swallowed a man and spit out a missionary.

The image I love is Jonah rising from the slime, his pose similar to the painting of "The Birth of Venus" where beautiful Venus is depicted rising out of the ocean on a half-shell. Beautiful is a word that no one would have applied to Jonah. The artwork by Sandro Bottechelli is a thing of beauty; with Jonah it becomes a scene fitting for a distasteful movie. The image is awesome. I doubt that Jonah even tried to scrape the slimy vomit from his person. He probably wore it to Nineveh as a badge, a sign of the insult he had endured for their sake. When he took his first clear lungful of air, He must have found it to be a beautiful thing.

There, on the beach, probably in modern-day Syria, Jonah turned to walk east. He was going to Nineveh and he was going to preach, as God had told him to do in the beginning. This time, Jonah was ready. It was only four hundred miles to go and he had a message to bring to them.

Inside the whale, Jonah learned what he never wanted to admit about himself. But inside the whale, he had been in God's classroom. He emerged changed for the better although he looked the worse. He came out of that classroom with a tenderized spirit, his spirit softened by solitude and secretions.

And I will forever wonder, "What did the whale think about all this?"

Chapter Four

Continued:

Considering Jonah, Section Three

Because of the similarities between Jonah 1:1-2 and 3:1-2, let us first review the opening two verses in the Book of Jonah. The first chapter reads: "**1**¹ The word of the Lord came to Jonah the son of Amittai saying, ²Arise, go to Nineveh, that great city, and cry against it; for their wickedness is come up before me."

God is a wonderfully patient teacher; Jonah was a reluctant, resistant, and rebellious student. The Lord, as if undisturbed that the one who had been called had tried to flee that calling, calmly repeated his message. A good boss, coach, manager, or whoever is in charge will often speak calmly to a worker who has messed up in some way. The only real difference in the two messages is that this second time when God spoke, He didn't mention the wickedness of the city. Another important distinction is that the first time Jonah heard the message, he was well dressed; the second time he heard the voice, he had whale vomit dripping off him.

We read:

3¹ And the word of the LORD came unto Jonah the second time, saying,

Believe this: Jonah was much more receptive to God's message than he was the first time. He may well have originally rationalized the message; the second time it was an order he was going to obey.

² Arise, go unto Nineveh, that great city, and preach unto it the preaching that I bid thee.

The LORD didn't mention the wickedness of Nineveh this time, but only that Jonah should "cry against it." Jonah was instructed to "preach unto it the preaching that I bid thee." Jonah was willing this time; the words would come and he would proclaim that message.

"Arise. Go . . ." says the LORD to Jonah, not arising from the comforts of his home or as the captain called to him from sleeping in the ship, but this time to arise from a pool of indescribable slime. Jonah arose and went. Jonah still did not want to go, but this time he would go and deliver that message. I can imagine

Jonah's anger; he was already prejudiced (the word source here is "pre-judged") against the people of Nineveh, but now he would probably blame them for his entire whale experience. His anger and outrage would show in every word and every gesture he made. It was a rare opportunity for Jonah to show all his indignant rage while still doing the work that God's called him to do.

³ So Jonah arose, and went unto Nineveh, according to the word of the LORD. Now Nineveh was an exceeding great city of three days' journey.

This is the way it was supposed to be. The LORD said, "Arise. Go." Jonah arose, and went. It still wasn't Jonah's idea to go, especially to Nineveh, but the LORD said "Go" and Jonah went. But he didn't go as an over-educated Pharisee, a child of his father's teaching as he may have been at the time of his first invitation. This time he went as a man sent by God. He was a man with a purpose. He had been in God's classroom once; he had learned his lesson. The Jonah in Chapter Three has little in common with the Jonah of Chapter One.

Oh, but biblical scholars and skeptics go ecstatically crazy with the description of the size of Nineveh! They seem not to be at all impressed that Jonah covered the remaining four hundred miles without the help of a great fish, but they get tied up and argumentative on how big a city was if it could be described as a city of "three day's journey." Some claim it must be the circumference, meaning it would take

Jonah three days to walk around the outside wall, a distance of roughly sixty miles. "Too big," some say. Others surmise it would have taken Jonah three days to walk every street and alley to reach all the people. "Not big enough," others claim. If the population were 120,000 as it says later in Jonah, it would have been one of America's largest cities, ranking in the 200 largest cities in the United States. "Too many," some say; "Gross exaggeration," say others.

Nineveh, on the banks of the Tigris River, dates back to 5,000 B.C. But if I'd just walked 400 miles, a three-day walk through town would have seemed a very short distance unless I was very tired. But we don't know, so we'll just go on with the story.

⁴ And Jonah began to enter into the city a day's journey, and he cried, and said, "Yet forty days, and Nineveh shall be overthrown."

There are words that indicate time, often they are short words, but they set a stage we want to understand. The first word of the book of Jonah starts out with the word "Now." "Now" means present tense, now and at that moment. The LORD said it: God meant it. Later we hit "Then" and see it as a word to indicate past tense. In this verse we find another time word: "Yet." "Yet" is a word which here indicates the future tense. These are time words: Jonah 1:1 for "Now;" 2:2 for "Then;" and "Yet" in verse 3:4. They are clues to the reading of the story. Here in the message that Jonah brought to Nineveh, spoken in only eight words (five in the Hebrew text), Jonah cried out to them, "Yet forty days, and Nineveh shall be overthrown."

The number forty is fairly common in the Bible and carries with it a symbolic meaning. It rained for forty days in Noah's time. Forty was the number of years the Jews wandered in the wilderness. Moses was on Mount Sinai for forty days. It was forty years between Moses killing the Egyptian and his return to Egypt. Elijah hid for forty days. The spies were in Canaan for forty days. Later, Jesus was in the wilderness for forty days. Because the Jews have a special relationship with the number forty, when the LORD gave that number to him, Jonah understood the significance of it.

Jonah entered the city and cried, "Yet!" On his first day he cried out to them, "You have forty days before Nineveh is overthrown!" When Jonah preached, it was a message of vengeance. He cried "against" Nineveh, as he had been instructed in verse 1:2. To make his message more impactful, I do not believe that Jonah ever washed, nor did he ever change his clothes after his encounter with the great fish. I think he wanted the people to see what God can do to those who disobey. Jonah's message was more than the words the LORD had given him; much of the message was revealed by the image of the man who delivered it.

"The Medium is the Message," wrote Canadian sociologist Marshall McLuhan in 1967, taken from his book of a similar title. Jonah was a living, breathing, stinking example of the theme of McLuhan's message; his appearance seems to be part of the message. The people of Nineveh heard his words as they had heard many others, but when they saw him--they believed!

Undoubtedly they believed in part because of Jonah's displayed rage in not washing or changing; another aspect of Jonah's success in bringing God's message was the look in his eyes as he cried out to them.

When Jonah screamed at them in outrage, "Yet forty days! In forty days you're all gonna die! You deserve to die!" The people believed him! I wonder if he madly giggled with glee when he recited the message God had given him to deliver. They heard Jonah, but it was God they believed.

5 So the people of Nineveh believed God, and proclaimed a fast, and put on sackcloth, from the greatest of them even to the least of them.

The people of Nineveh believed God. Truly, when they heard Jonah, they believed God. Perhaps in part because of Jonah's look, the people proclaimed a fast and donned sackcloth, all of them. Did they do so in mock imitation of Jonah's dress and his look—gaunt and angry and fishy? Did they imitate him?

I can imagine the money that Jonah brought with him from Gath-Hepher was lost when he left the ship. It could have been that he begged his way to Nineveh, further enhancing his look and temper. When the people of Nineveh realized Jonah was angry but not crazy, the weight of his words increased.

6 For word came unto the king of Nineveh, and he arose from his throne, and he laid his robe from him, and covered him with sackcloth, and sat in ashes.

This is not the behavior of a king. This is the behavior of a troubled man, in this case a troubled leader who heard the words of a prophet and opened his eyes. Was it the first time the king saw the sins of his people and of his own evil? There had been a mad man, a Hebrew, in the king's own kingdom who preached a strange message. The mad man looked and smelled and acted as if he slept in a pile of dead fish. Somehow the king of Nineveh heard the message, but it wasn't only the words he heard, it was the messenger who terrified him.

Then came a second fear: how could that madman have known these things? The king probably heard something in the message of that madman that spoke of things that no one but the king should have known. It would have been then the truth occurred to the king: Jonah may have seemed to be only a madman, but he was a crazy man who'd been sent by God! There was a revelation that took place in the heart of the king and he repented. He stepped away from the royal throne that marked him superior to all other men. He stripped off the royal garb, leaving behind his royal robes as he wrapped himself in sackcloth and sat in ashes, a place from which you can go no lower. This was the last place to be, the lowest point.

Now imagine his servants and those who ruled under him finding him in such a state. At first they must have thought him mad, for somehow the words he'd heard from Jonah's lips caught fire in the king's heart to cause him to repent. From the ashes and sackcloth came a new fire of passion, the king ordered changes in his kingdom. The king had repented. Now it was his duty to help his people.

The king's story is a precursor of what happened with King Nebuchadnezzar during the time of the captivity.

7 And he caused it to be proclaimed and published through Nineveh by the decree of the king and his nobles, saying, Let neither man nor beast, herd nor flock, taste any thing: let them not feed, nor drink water:

It is possible that the king was also the major religious figure in Nineveh. If that was true, then when he decreed something, there was a double reason to obey him. "By Proclamation of the King" are words that cause change. It is politically expedient to do the bidding of the king, and sometimes it is wise to do so— not for the sake of political cleverness, but because the king has spoken the truth. Did not the king take the words of that crazed Hebrew prophet, Jonah, and command the people to repent? By decree, a legal writ, the king (and his nobles, none of whom wanted to cross the king) had it proclaimed and published across the kingdom, "Let neither man nor beast, herd or flock, taste any thing. Let them not feed. Let them not drink, not even water!"

The people heeded the decree. As ordered, they turned to God. You can be certain many made that transition only by mouthing the words. However, sometimes words are enough to cause change in the hearer's heart. As the king led them, so did they follow his new behavior. Dressed in sackcloth, their animal likewise, they cried out in a loud voice to God. They repented of their sins.

⁸ But let man and beast be covered with sackcloth, and cry mightily unto God: yea, let them turn every one from his evil way, and from the violence that is in their hands.

They dared not call him LORD. They cried "unto God" but not unto the LORD. It is possible that Jonah withheld the LORD's personal name and just gave the descriptive name of God. The prayer of the people was better focused than that of the sailors', each of whom prayed to "his god." They must have done something right because God heard them. Nor did they merely cover themselves with sackcloth and cry with great depth as those in danger might pray to God. God heard them because of who He is, not because of what they did. Mercy is of the LORD, as is Salvation.

They repented. "Yea, let them turn every one from his evil ways, and from the violence that is in their hands." This is interesting: "Let them turn," plural; "every one," singular; "from his evil," singular; "and the violence that is in their hands," plural. They knew of the need to change their ways and, with Jonah as catalyst, repentance happened. Jonah didn't do it; it was the work of the LORD and the LORD 's doing. It is an admirable thing, that an entire people group, nation, city, or even a church might all examine themselves and then repent. Real change is fairly rare; yet here is an entire city changed.

Repentance is not resignation to change. It is the process of actually changing. And how does one change? By going to God. People turn to God not because God is good but because they have done evil. To whom or where else could they turn? There is no one else. What was it that Jonah said in his prayer from the belly of the great fish? "Salvation is of the LORD." And so it remains.

The crux of Jonah's message to the people of Nineveh was not that they would perish in forty days, although I'm sure he thought that was the most important part of his message. The real heart of his message was this: Salvation is of the LORD!

⁹ Who can tell if God will turn and repent, and turn away from his fierce anger, that we perish not?

It was the king's question, undoubtedly repeated by the people of Nineveh many times. It was a good question, this "Who can tell?" We don't always know, but when we need an answer, we are more ready to try things. The sackcloth and ashes may have helped, but it was their hearts calling on God that provided the solution they needed.

There are many sad theologians who try to convince us that God does not ever turn and repent, that miracles are a thing of the past, and because God is omniscient and knows all things past, present, and future; nothing will ever really change. They would say that whoever (God) knows all, such a one never needs to repent of anything. Those rigid theologians are probably wrong most of the time. God did not repent because he was wrong; God "repented" because the people finally repented. The judge can show mercy even when the law would condemn; likewise, God shows mercy to us even in the face of the law that can rightfully condemn us.

Nineveh later fell again into her evil ways and was eventually destroyed. We will never know what good came from Jonah's time there. We should consider the story of the LORD visiting Abraham on the plains of Mamre to see an example of how the presence of a few can save the lives of many. In the Genesis 18:20-32 account, Abraham pleaded with the LORD to not destroy them all. I do not believe the sparing of the people of Nineveh was in vain, but there is no proof and there are no words to confirm that. Who knows how many repented and remained changed? How many of them were saved?

10 And God saw their works, that they turned from their evil way; and God repented of the evil, that he had said that he would do unto them; and he did it not.

The basis of the word "repent" means, literally, "to turn around or to breathe again." It's a word that speaks of a renewed life, of the change that happens when we begin to listen to God. In this case, God granted them an extended life. And why would God repent? Because the people wanted to but didn't know how, so God showed them. It was almost as if God repented for them, and not necessarily that God is the one who repented. And for whom did Jesus die? The answers are the same.

We pray to a God, the LORD, who we know hears our prayers and responds. Apparently God also responds to our words and our works, our intentions and our love. God hears the individual and the group prayer. God is God; God will do what God will do. It is not for us to judge or to try to manipulate judgments. God judges, sometimes with mercy and sometimes with power. We repent; sometimes God does likewise.

That which "he had said that he would do unto the people; and he did it not." This changed Jonah's future. Did the people accept it was God who saved them or that Jonah was a false prophet who should be stoned?

Imagine you have been in an accident in which someone died. It was your fault, but not through negligence or excessive action. You and you alone are guilty. Your lawyer tells you that you could be sentenced to fifteen years in prison and you are at the mercy of the judge. The judge condemns your role in the accident but then sentences you to one year of probation. The judge knew the law but yet repented of the law, thereby showing you, a sinner, mercy. God did likewise for the people of Nineveh.

As in the Balaam story (Numbers 22) where the prophet was hired to curse the Hebrews but he did not, so too did Jonah ultimately do what God wanted of him, but only after a series of trials.

These are lovely words, "And he did it not." These are life-giving words. The gods of men would always condemn because they have no mercy. God repented of what could have happened and showed the people mercy. Repentance can do that. Sincere repentance is often the only defense we have. A contrite heart is sometimes the only strength we have.

Jonah wasn't expecting that outcome. He could not believe that Nineveh would truly repent and that God would accept it. I can imagine these words being the worst words Jonah ever heard: "Nineveh lives!"

Chapter Four
Continued:

Considering Jonah, Section Four

4¹ But it displeased Jonah exceedingly, and he was very angry.

On the fortieth day the sun arose on Nineveh and the merciful judgment of God shown upon the people. For a man like Jonah who'd grown up with the faith of his father, thinking he was flawless, this would not have been a good day. As a child he was a product of his father's discipline and expectations. We can be sure he learned very early that it was important to protect and defend one's reputation. I can imagine his father driving that dictum into his son's head, "Above all, protect your reputation." Now, in the face of the repentance of Nineveh, it was time for Jonah to repent.

Protecting himself may have been the motivating force behind Jonah's attempt to flee to Tarshish rather than serve in Nineveh. But Jonah didn't flee the second time; instead he boldly marched into Nineveh and announced, gleefully, that Nineveh was going to collapse, "You are all going to die!" I imagine Jonah shrieking, his finger pointing at each individual, as he laughed at the thought. God gave him the freedom to speak against the city for all its wickedness. Jonah, never forgetting the hell he went through to get there, pronounced the word of God against them.

Then God "repented!" God's mercy is wonderful, but Jonah thought he was left looking like a fool, a madman, and a liar. His reputation had been crushed. He would have failed his father and himself. He was exceedingly displeased. He was angry. The more he thought about it, the more furious he became! God had used and abused him, then left him looking like an idiot. Jonah raged at his God. Jonah couldn't tolerate the fact that God wouldn't follow through on the plan of what Jonah thought God should do.

2 And he prayed unto the LORD, and said, I pray thee, O LORD, was not this my saying, when I was yet in my country? Therefore I fled before unto Tarshish: for I knew that thou art a gracious God, and merciful, slow to anger, and of great kindness, and repentest thee of the evil.

When Jonah prayed to God, he called him LORD. As the prayer from the belly of the great fish was earnest and humbled, this prayer now was much more like the old Jonah. Gone is the beseeching and sense of surrender from Jonah when he was trapped in the darkness. Here is a prayer of self-righteous indignation, explaining his actions as if they were the only truth. Rationalization is a form of self-deception and it is a form of lying, something we say to justify our actions. Jonah's prayer was a prayer of self-justification to his LORD.

My wife does this. We'd get on a plane bound for Africa and she'd announce, thirty minutes into the flight, that she'd forgotten the binoculars. She says, "I knew I was going to do that!" No, she didn't; if she'd known that she was going to forget them, she wouldn't have left them. It's an example of rationalization, pretending you could have prevented what happened by pretending that by doing something before it happened, she would thereby have prevented what happened from happening. But the sad part is that I knew she was going to say that. No, I didn't, but that's what rationalization is.

Hear Jonah's three rationalizations in this single verse: 1) This is what I said before I left home; 2) That's why I fled to Tarshish; and 3) I know you are gracious, merciful, slow to anger, kind, and capable to REPENTEST THEE OF THE EVIL.

No, he didn't know that. The possibility was there, but he didn't know it or say it earlier. He fled Joppa because he was afraid, but later he explained to his LORD that he was really doing it to protect God's reputation. Jonah had preached judgment against Nineveh and then God relented; Jonah thought he would be seen as a false prophet because Nineveh was not destroyed in forty days. Afterwards he claimed he knew that's what would happen and that was why he'd fled. He wasn't afraid to blame God for it. Jonah again fled, but this time only to a nearby place where he could watch the city. When Nineveh wasn't destroyed, Jonah was furious. He would have considered the repentance of the people of Nineveh to be superficial. Jonah was angry at the success of his preaching. He was angry at everything.

Jonah raged against God because God had shown mercy and repented, unmindful that God had done the same thing, on a smaller scale, when the great fish spit him out. It really does no good to rage against God, for God will forever do what God will do.

The humbled Jonah of Chapter 2, the hopeful man praying to his LORD from inside the belly of the whale, was a different Jonah from the pessimistic one who now raged against his LORD. But the LORD of Jonah remained constantly merciful.

³ Therefore now, O LORD, take, I beseech thee, my life from me; for it is better for me to die than to live.

"Take my life!" Jonah prays, talking to his LORD, eager to show his willingness to die more for the sake of his own vanity than he was willing to die in service to the LORD. Now that's not what he thought he was telling God, but the truth of his prayer is not deeply buried. How vain is the one who can say, "They may laugh at me," and prefer death to life? Jonah knew it is almost impossible to re-establish a soiled reputation. To be laughed at was more than Jonah could stand.

The LORD used Jonah only after Jonah was prepared. Why did Jonah have to go through all those trials and insults? I suppose it is because if Jonah had just walked up and spoken to the people of Nineveh, his heart and soul wouldn't have been on fire with the message. But after what he went through and how he looked, God had prepared him to speak to the people of Nineveh with a passion Jonah could only have found when he was inside the great fish. The experience gave him focus.

God knows what to do. God knew what it would take for the people to respond to Jonah. The promise to destroy Nineveh, that great and wicked city, was true, but God foresaw that a character like Jonah was needed to save the city. Jonah did exactly as God knew he would; Jonah performed the miracle and yet he did not see the miracle. All Jonah could see was that the words he spoke were false and the lie could destroy his reputation. He did not see that his words changed a people and the fate of a great city. He whined when he should have stood in awe at the understanding and work of the LORD.

"Let me die," screamed the slowest and most vain of all the prophets, whining to the very end.

4 Then said the LORD, Doest thou well to be angry?

I can imagine the LORD, Adonai, the Creator of the Seas and Lands, YHWH, God, smirking at Jonah's vanity. It looks like a question, "Doest thou well to be angry?" But it is really a statement. The wickedness of Nineveh looked minor in comparison to the vanity of Jonah.

"Really, Jonah, is this worth dying for?" the Lord pointed to the city and watched as Jonah looked up and saw the city alive.

⁵ So Jonah went out of the city, and sat on the east side of the city, and there made him a booth, and sat under it in the shadow, till he might see what would become of the city.

Sometimes there is no answer to give. Apparently Jonah looked to where God indicated, then turned and walked away. He'd never been told to stay in Nineveh, only to go to that city and preach. He had done that.

It must have been the dawn of the fortieth day when Jonah hoped his heavy words of prophecy would still come true and the city of Nineveh would be destroyed. In case this was the day, Jonah cleared out of the city proper and went to the east, away from town, and built himself a bit of a lean-to to protect himself from the sun. It was there he intended to sit and watch God destroy Nineveh, or it was there he intended to die. He had faithfully carried out the word that the Lord had told him to deliver, the message of God. He felt he should expect nothing less than a fulfillment of those words. He thought it was a promise to him personally and he expected God to keep the promise of what Jonah thought those words meant. Utterly frustrated at his God's behavior, Jonah sat down, useless and inert, and waited for God to do what was promised.

⁶ And the Lord God prepared a gourd, and made

it to come up over Jonah, that it might be a shadow over his head, to deliver him from his grief. So Jonah was exceeding glad of the gourd.

The pouting prophet sat in his little shelter and waited to see if God would honor him, a true son of the Hebrews, a messenger of God's word to the people of Nineveh, or if God would perjure himself and let the wickedness of the city go unpunished, allowing the evilness to live and breed. Jonah saw this as being a test of God's character. He could not see that it was he himself who was on trial.

The LORD is a magnificent teacher, knowing each student well. The lesson prepared for Jonah that day took the shape of a fast-growing plant, probably a gourd plant, that grew up overnight and spread it's leaves over Jonah, better shading him than Jonah's little shelter did. Jonah found comfort in the plant, understanding this was a bit of the honor he deserved for his work in Nineveh. Obviously, he understood it to show God was with him and would shelter him on the day the city of Nineveh was to be delivered to the fate it deserved. In the shade and in a cool breeze, Jonah sat and waited.

7 But God prepared a worm when the morning rose the next day, and it smote the gourd that it withered.

What was the next day to Jonah was still in the LORD's "Now" in the first verse of this book. The generation of the plant was a single day in man's eye while the generation of man is but a day in God's eye. It is all so relative. God's "now" is eternal.

The lessons of God often follow the word "But." Here again the "But God" was teaching a most reluctant student. This was not the LORD and not Adonai, but it was God who then delivered the punch line to the joke, the summary of all the lessons and was, ultimately, the conclusion of the story. A worm, like a spiritual termite, prepared long before Jonah ever considered going to Nineveh, awoke and ate the root of the gourd plant. Cut off from the nutrients and the structural support it needed to survive, the quick-growing plant also proved to be a quick-dying plant. It withered, a victim of the worm. It was all as the LORD intended.

8 **And it came to pass, when the sun did arise, that God prepared a vehement east wind; and the sun beat upon the head of Jonah, that he fainted, and wished in himself to die, and said, "It is better for me to die than to live."**

Oh, it was such a lovely lesson plan that God had for Jonah. The plant withered, leaving the inadequate shelter that Jonah built for himself exposed. Then the sun arose hot and angry. Immediately following the sunrise was a vehement east wind that blew hot from the desert and dried up the withering plant. The wind probably tore apart Jonah's little shelter. The hot, drying wind and intense sun beat upon Jonah's head, so much so that he grew faint. He watched the city on the forty-first day and still it lived. He thought his work had been in vain.

Jonah had had enough. After the word of the LORD had first come into his life, then came the storm, followed by the great fish, then the plant, and finally the worm. Jonah was slow to figure out that things in his life were going to be done in God's way, not his own. This is the third time he was ready to die, first on the ship as he was thrown overboard, now twice as he looked down upon a thriving Nineveh.

He grew faint from the heat and drying wind. The wind, known as a sirocco, can bring temperatures of forty-five degrees Celsius, above a hundred Fahrenheit, with almost zero percent humidity. Knowing the LORD was still hearing him, he repeated his line, "It is better for me to die than to live." This was his conclusion. He had tried to serve the LORD but he proved incapable. He tried to run away but could not. He warned a people they would die in forty days and they did not. Finally he built a shelter for himself and it blew away. He was a total failure and saw no future hope for himself. "It is better for me to die than to live," he said, thinking everything he had ever tried to do for his LORD was completely wrong.

Jonah had finally lost hope.

9 And God said to Jonah, Doest thou well to be angry for the gourd? And he said, I do well to be angry, even unto death.

God said, "Oh Jonah, are you right to be angry even for the plant?"

Jonah would have whined, "Yes, for the gourd and

for the heat and the wind and the wickedness of the city. Don't forget being tossed overboard in the middle of a gale or the days spent in the Sheol of that great fish. I have been mocked and humiliated, insulted, and accused of the crimes you have committed. I have been lied to by my LORD, and yes, even the drying up of the gourd! I have earned the right to be angry. Yes, I am angry, even unto my death!" Jonah could have said, but he did not. Finally he sat down quietly and waited.

Jonah was always quick to judge everything according to his self-righteousness. Finally it seemed to him that even his God had turned against him. There was no place else to go and nothing to do except to die.

10 Then said the LORD, Thou hast had pity on the gourd, for the which thou hast not laboured, neither madest it grow; which came up in a night, and perished in a night:

"Then said the LORD," not merely God but the LORD, YHWH, Adonai, "The gourd was never yours. You never planted it, you never labored over it, and you did not make it grow. It sprang up in the night and perished in the day, but it was never yours. Yet you have pity and grief for the plant."

11 And should not I spare Nineveh, that great city, wherein are more than six-score thousand persons that cannot discern between their right hand and their left hand; and also much cattle?

The story ends with a question mark, as does the US National Anthem. It means the story isn't over yet. It is right that the Book of Jonah ends with a question mark. The story isn't over yet because we, in our own petty ways, are still living out the Jonah story. Our refusal to read the Bible is not unlike Jonah's attempted flight to Tarshish. The story isn't over because somewhere in our lives lurks our whales, ready to return us to the path we should walk. The young have whales they have yet to find; the elderly probably can identify theirs easily. We are all different and yet we are all the same.

In Jonah's silence the LORD spoke the final words of the Book of Jonah. The LORD said this, "Jonah, you idiot, it was I who spared Nineveh. It wasn't you. In that city were more than 120,000 people who know nothing, not even the difference between their right hand and their left, or right from wrong. And do not forget the cattle."

In silence Jonah heard the lesson and apparently he finally understood: it's the LORD's world. God will do what God will do and to that end Jonah needs to remain in grateful awe, as he claimed to be when he was home in Gath-hepher.

In the Book of Jonah, the LORD spoke first and the LORD spoke last. This is as it should be. Jonah and the LORD were not friends, not good-buddies; they were more like the rich boss and the field hand. But they loved each other. I think sometimes God laughed at Jonah, and I think that Jonah always knew he was loved.

This is an important detail: No matter how foolish he sounded or acted, Jonah was always a believer. It is the reason he was able to become that much-praised "servant of God" (2 Kings 14:25). Let us be likewise.

And the rest was silence.

Chapter Five
Considering Jonah

APPENDICES

May you not have gotten so wrapped up in this Jonah story that you missed its message.

The following are not Biblical endings of the story of Jonah. These are the works of this author trying to present possibilities, nothing more. If there had been a fifth chapter to the Book of Jonah, it may have been one of these three offerings. There is no theology involved here. These are the writings of the storyteller telling a story, trying to share some of the joy of the Book of Jonah. That is all that it is, that and nothing more. Yet they are more, for these endings are intended to give a flavor to the story, to make the wondrous tale more memorable. Please take these endings with a grain of salt or two aspirin, depending on your need.

Ending One:

One of the possibilities regarding the point and purpose of the Book of Jonah is that it is the silliest story ever penned.

Ending Two:

And Jonah faithfully served the LORD his God all his days. He desired to write of the wonderful story of the life the LORD had given him and of the all the miracles that God had accomplished through him, yet forever it seemed as if God said to him, "Not yet, Jonah. Do not write yet." And so Jonah waited, serving God, growing older.

It is a dangerous thing to serve a God who has a righteous sense of humor.

For then, one day, the word of LORD came to Jonah again and said, "Sit. Write. Now." That was all, but Jonah knew this was his chance to tell the world of his greatness in serving God, of all his desires to become a faithful servant and powerful man of God. He could tell how it had all come to fruition. And so, finally, Jonah sat down and began to write.

In one hour he wrote the beginning of his life, his embarrassing opening as a prophet of God. He wanted the world to know that it had not always been easy. He wanted the world to know that he had once been swallowed by a great fish and then vomited on the shore because God was not merely God of Israel but of the entire world, of all creation. It was good to start his story humbly.

So Jonah wrote his first words on the epic that would forever label him one of the great prophets and servants of God. Having penned his opening about how his ministry had begun in Nineveh, a sudden pain like an ocean swell swept through his chest and Jonah, the son of Amittai, died before he could write his story.

He was furious.

He turned to God and asked with the same kind of temper he'd shown in the beginning of his ministry, "What have YOU done? I only had a chance to write about the opening of my work! People will read that and laugh!"

To this God responded, "Jonah, your life as a prophet is documented. Be assured." And then God left him. As God walked away, Jonah thought, but he was not sure, that he heard God chuckling.

Everyone in heaven read Jonah's short account. They truly loved it. They read it and they laughed while Jonah fumed. He was often seen in heaven stomping around heavily, snorting and snarling, angry and without any recourse.

In time the Messiah was born. It was an event greatly celebrated in heaven. From the edge of heaven looking down, they all watched the baby grow to become a child and the child to be a man. All of heaven understood that God's plan was perfect; none in heaven understood what this special child had to do with the redemption of those sinful people but they believed. They, while they could not comprehend the plan, trusted God.

Among the many watchers was Jonah.

All of heaven watched the final week of the life of Jesus. They saw the betrayal, but God prevented them from intervening. They saw the mock trial and beating that the Christ took; they watched him being nailed to the cross, mocked, tormented and tortured, but God would not interfere, nor would God let them intervene. Heaven stood silent as Jesus died.

Jonah was beside himself. He was silent and he was furious, for this was the second time he thought God had failed, first in his own life and again in the wrongful death of Jesus, the Messiah.

Most of heaven wandered away, saddened and confused, but Jonah sat and watched, and watched even beyond the end of the story. On the first day of the week he witnessed the resurrection of Jesus, returning from the dead with the saints. It was marvelous. While most of heaven rejoiced, Jonah cried.

He turned and was surprised to find God standing beside him. Jonah looked up and through tears and a choking voice said, "Sir, His death and resurrection, that was, that was, that was my story, wasn't it."

God looked at him and nodded.

"Sir, it wasn't my words that were prophesy, it was my life!"

God nodded.

"My time in the whale, my being cast out, leading the city to repentance . . ."

God nodded.

In joy, Jonah wept.

From that day forth, in all of heaven, there is said to be no one happier in all of heaven than Jonah.

Ending Three:

Option number three is the purpose of this book. As you may have suspected, perhaps by the loose writing style and freedom of thought of this author, this author is an alcoholic. That's why Jonah's home of Gath-hepher as the site of the winepress, his name possibly meaning someone slightly intoxicated, and the concept of being swallowed by something he couldn't resist all contributed to this unique and humorous study in the wonderful tale of Jonah. The worm that ate the gourd root was also the worm that destroyed many vineyards, the source of wine. Everything in the story reminds me of my own alcoholic addictions, something I've never overcome or defeated. I am sober now, today. I pray I am tomorrow, as well.

Whenever the Rev. Dr. Martin Luther King Jr. spoke, every sermon and every lesson turned into a forum for freedom and equality for all people. That was his passion, his understanding of the world. He optimistically dreamt of a better world.

My passion, my understanding of the world is based upon the view of eyes too long blurred by alcohol. I have been sober more than thirty-five years now, and yet I still crave that magic elixir which made, it seemed to me, my life more complete. Then, I rejoiced in the freedom alcohol gave me while, in fact, my entire life was falling apart.

The name of my whale was alcohol. My bottle was the whale. My image of myself in regard to the Jonah story is being inside the bottle, unable to get out. He, whose name is Jonah (from the root meaning bubbly) and hailing from Gath-hepher (the place of the winepress), may have become a prophet only when he put that beast behind him, found sobriety, and preached the word of God. My Jonah, by my reasoning, was an alcoholic. Is that true?

How utterly ridiculous!

No. Of course not.

Yet, allow me to retell the story of Jonah to you. It goes like this:

I know Jonah very well . . . (My story continues in Chapter Three, page 18, just under the heading: JONAH).

Chapter Six

SO, WHAT IS YOUR WHALE?

This final section deals not with Jonah, but with us. We all have Whales in our past, in the same sense that we're all our own Jonahs. But these Whales that we have in our lives, past or present, are not always a bad thing. They help us identify and define ourselves. Generally, they are things, people, or events that have ended up redirecting our lives, usually without our consent, onto paths we'd never have otherwise traveled.

My Whale was, of course, alcohol and we don't need to dwell upon that, but I am aware that I'm always conscious of it lurking behind me. Sometimes it whispers my name; always it reminds me of the good times I had without ever recalling any of the bad. My doctor once asked me if I'd had anything to drink that year and I answered, "No, and proof of that is that I'm still alive." Also worth noting, that evil scourge of alcohol delivered me with as much dignity as did the Whale as it puked Jonah onto the beach. Like and unlike Jonah, I became a missionary. I am now retired, happily married and utterly amazed at how well my life turned out. The Whale was a voyage, the book is a journey, and the life is mine.

But again, what is your Whale? There are some Whales we don't or can't talk about. It is good that we don't have to wander through Nineveh covered with dried Whale vomit while testifying what things our Whale had done to us, as if it were an insult. With time, we may come to realize our Whales were a blessing, but that's generally true only if we have left them behind.

One of the ugliest Whales I know about is Betrayal. When your trust has been crushed, when you've felt your spirit break by someone you loved and trusted; that's an ugly Whale. When your kids lie to you and spend your money; that's a nasty Whale. Molested, I cannot begin to comprehend that Whale; I don't know how to forgive that. The hit-and-run driver who leaves you crippled. The drunk who has killed your family. Whales, we have these beasts in our past that don't go away and yet they shaped our lives.

How many times do you think Jonah woke from dreams of those three days trapped and hopeless in the hot, black, smelly, noisy innards of the Whale? How many soldiers wake screaming from memories of the war? How many times do you wake in a panic from the memories of your Whale, your heart pounding and palms sweaty? My Whale is still with me to remind me never to relax my vigil. No, we don't forget our Whales.

I have lived with the Book of Jonah for over thirty years. The first time I read it was during my first year of full-time sobriety, I really connected with it. The first sermon I ever gave was on Jonah. Thirty-five years later, when I sat down to type the fourth chapter of this book I opened no reference books but *Strong's Concordance*. I typed parts of the book with my eyes closed, my mind racing through the story I knew so well. It remains a story I lived in my own life. The story version of Jonah in Chapter Three was written years ago.

Our Whales are behind us, we don't have to look back to know that. We live in their shadows, but we need to leave them. We all have in our past some great, looming, hulking memories. We would not be who we are today without them. Jonah is at his best at the moment the Whale casts him back into the world; he is at his worst when he sits alone with expectations of others (here hoping that God would destroy Nineveh). Oh, Jonah and I have so much in common!

Alcohol made me who I am today. It's not something I am proud of, but it's real. And because of that I almost inadvertently started Alcoholic Anonymous meetings in Tanzania that are still running. Eighteen years sober at that point, I still needed AA meetings in a place where there were none. Behold, that which I needed I started. Now, years later when I may not even be a memory in anyone's memory there, the meetings are still running and spreading, doing good. Later we started Narcotics Anonymous to meet the needs. The AA group in Nairobi, Kenya came down and spent three days with us learning how the NA group had started. When they went back, they started their own. Without my Whale, that would not have been possible.

A mother whose child had been killed by a drunk driver began MADD, Mothers Against Drunk Drivers. There are countless numbers of good things God has done using what people have learned and started because of their Whales. Our Whales change us.

Like Jonah whose Whale changed his course of direction and then delivered him to where he should be, my Whale turned out to be a blessing. It takes years to recognize that. That which once I thought was evil has turned out to be a blessing. What a surprise!

It turns out the evil was not in the Whale, it was in me. It was not the alcohol; I was the evil agent! It was how I coped with it that made the difference. Not always even realizing what I was doing, God used my Whale experience for the good of others.

So, what's your Whale?

And, my final thought which may or may not be true, but I'm coming to the conclusion that not only am I Jonah, but I AM MY OWN WHALE too! Who or what is my Whale? I am.

LIMITED BIBLIOGRAPHY

BOOKS USED IN THE WRITING OF JONAH: WHAT'S YOUR WHALE?

Strong, James. STRONG'S EXHAUSTIVE CONCORDANCE OF THE BIBLE. Abingdon Press, 1890.

REFERENCES ON HAND BUT NOT CITED

Bloomquist, Daniel R. *THE BIBLE: God's Rescue Plan for the Human Race*. Xulon Press, Florida. 2015.

Calvin, Johannes. Trans. By John Owen. *TWELVE MINOR PROPHETS*. "Prophet Jonah." Baker Book House, Grand Rapids. 1993.

Devine, James D. *FIND GOD'S WILL FOR YOU*. G/L Regal Books, Glendale, CA. n.d.

Ellul, Jacques. *THE JUDGMENT OF JONAH*. Eerdmans, Grand Rapids. 1971.

Epp, Theodore H. *JONAH: A Message for Our Times*. Back to the Bible Broadcast, Lincoln. 1960.

Fretheim, Terence E. *THE MESSAGE OF JONAH: A Theological Commentary*. Augsburg Publishing, Minneapolis. 1977.

Force, Maynard A. *JONAH SPEAKS*. Lutheran Bible Institute, Minneapolis. 1950.

Lifshitz, Ze'ev Haim. *THE PARADOX OF HUMAN EXISTENCE: A commentary on the Book of Jonah*. Jason Aronson, Inc., Northvale, New Jersey, 1994.

Meier, Norbert R. *JONAH: The Unwilling Missionary*. Northwest Publishing house, Milwaukee. 1972.

Merton, Thomas. *THE SIGNS OF JONAS*. Harvest/HBJ Book, New York. 1953.

Pickard, William M. *RATHER DIE THAN LIVE—JONAH*. Global Ministries, Untied Methodist Church, New York. 1974.

Pusey, E. B. "Jonah" in *Barnes on the Old Testament, The Minor Prophets: a Commentary, vol. 1.* Baker Book House, Grand Rapids. 1973.

Spina, Frank Anthony. *THE FAITH OF THE OUTSIDER: Exclusion and Inclusion in the Biblical Story*. Eerdman's Publishing, Grand Rapids. 2005.

Walton, John. *JONAH: Bible Study Commentary*. Zondervan, Grand Rapids. 1982

Weiss, G. Christian. *WRONG-WAY JONAH*. Back to the Bible Broadcast, Lincoln. 1967.

Other available books by Marvin Kananen include:

Short Stories:

BAD THEOLOGY: Short Stories Meant to Shake the Rigid and Challenge the Spineless.

WILD PITCHES: 33 & 1/3 Baseball Stories: It's a record.

THE PERFECT PLANET and Other Stories. Science Fiction.

Novels:

SHADOWLINE: (based on Joseph Conrad's *The Shadow-Line*). Science Fiction.

MAKING GENESIS: Growing Old with a Bang.

WALKING WITH BASHO: An Inspirational Tale.

Inspirational:

THE CLOUD OF THE UNKNOWING: Paraphrased & Comprehendible: a new translation.

Missionary Books:

JEANNMARV'S AFRICA 2013: Afoot and Lighthearted: Tanzania and Ireland.

JEANNMARV'S AFRICA 2015: A Book of Blogs from Tanzania.

ABOUT THE AUTHOR:

Marvin Kananen is a Christian (albeit proof sometimes seems to be lacking). Now retired, Kananen has taught elementary school, high school, and university level students. In his lifetime he has fished commercially, long-shored, was the backdoor man at Easy Rider, done security work, taught incoming university freshmen students how to write papers at an academic level, pastored a church (for 22 months before they fired him), wrote 5 crossword puzzle books for Baker Book House and 1 for Halo Press (a division of Ottenheimer), wrote a biography and rewrote a study on Ezekiel. He was an editor for the Africa Theological Journal at Makumira University in Tanzania, was one of the founding instructors at Makumira University College (MUCO-Tanzania). He ended his career as an English teacher in 2010 as a missionary among the Maasai and teaching at the Maasae Girls Lutheran Secondary School (MGLSS) for his last twelve working years. At Saint Andrew's Lutheran Church, he currently co-teaches the "Jean and Marvin Theology-Heresy Lutheran Comedy Hour" every Sunday morning at 7:15 a.m., a time when fewer people are likely to be damaged. He is, by the way, a compulsive writer, having filled 154 journals (30,500 pages) in his twelve years in Tanzania. Surprisingly and wonderfully so, he is happily married, canoes, fishes, and lives in Bellevue, Washington.

31,191 words.

Made in the USA
Charleston, SC
14 August 2016